A Walk Through The

YORKSHIRE DALES

He had trudged through Yorkshire Dales,
Among the rocks and winding scars,
Where deep and low the hamlets lie
Beneath their little patch of sky
And little lot of stars.

William Wordsworth

Rising car ownership, improved roads, more free
time and changing lifestyles are fuelling a leisure
explosion that now brings some 10 million trips to the
Dales Park each year.

Richard Harvey, National Park Officer, 1991

A Walk Through The
YORKSHIRE DALES

by W.R. Mitchell

 DALESMAN

The Dalesman Publishing Company Ltd,
Clapham, Lancaster, LA2 8EB

First published 1992

ISBN: 1 85568 047 5

Typeset by Lands Services, East Molesey, Surrey
Printed and bound by Biddles of Guildford, Surrey

CONTENTS

FOREWORD

By Robert Williamson, former Bishop of Bradford

ONE of the most pleasurable things about being Bishop of Bradford is that my diocese stretches north, leaving behind the mills and industry of the city, up into the open country and into the beauty of the Dales. No Bishop can have a more beautiful diocese; each village has its own character, its particular stories and very often a beautiful and historic parish church.

Those of us who have grown to love the Dales also love the *Dalesman* and W.R. Mitchell has been a guide, mentor and bedside companion to thousands of us. This volume brings the Dales alive in his own endearing way, and I am sure that the tales he tells will be recounted many times over by others as they follow his footsteps.

I recently went on a "Pastoral Pilgrimage", walking through the Dales and visiting all the rural churches in my diocese. How I wish I had read these pages before I set out. What a wealth of information and "colour" I would have had at my command. However, I take comfort from realising that history and folklore are still in the making, and I could name other characters who I have met to stand alongside those you will read about in this volume.

Having read *A Walk through the Yorkshire Dales* my appetite is whetted once again, and the walking boots are being cleaned ... Who knows, we may meet up in some country pub in these magnificent Dales and swap a few stories that we first came across in this gem of a book.

†Robert Bradford

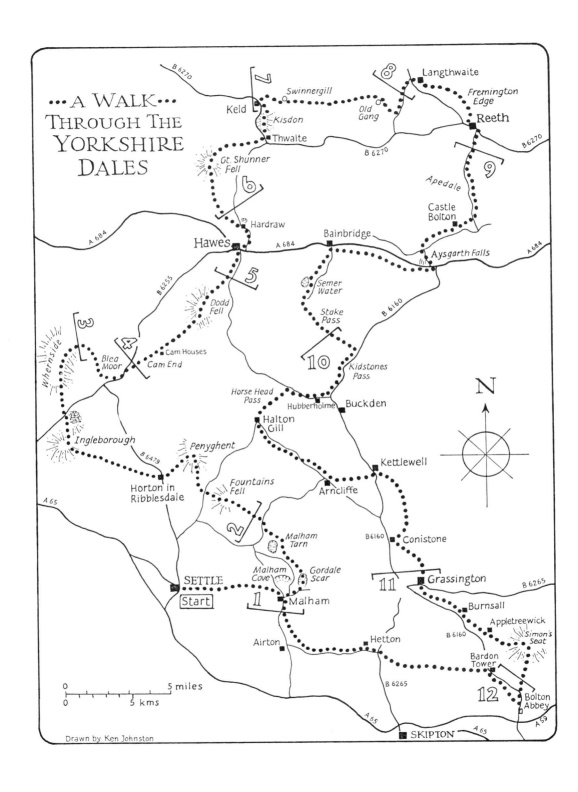

···A WALK···
THROUGH THE
YORKSHIRE
DALES

N

0   5 miles
0   5 kms

Drawn by Ken Johnston

B 6270

Swinnergill

Langthwaite

8

Fremington
Edge

Keld

Kisdon

Old
Gang

Reeth

B 6270

7

Thwaite

B 6270

9

Gt. Shunner
Fell

Apedale

6

Castle
Bolton

Hardraw

Bainbridge

Aysgarth Falls

A 684

Hawes

A 684

A 684

B 6255

5

Semer
Water

B 6160

Dodd
Fell

Stake
Pass

3

4

Cam Houses

10

Kidstones
Pass

Whernside

Blea
Moor

Cam End

Horse Head
Pass

Hubberholme

Buckden

Ingleborough

Penyghent

Halton
Gill

Kettlewell

B 6479

Horton in
Ribblesdale

Fountains
Fell

Arncliffe

A 65

2

B 6160

Conistone

Malham
Tarn

11

Grassington

B 6265

Malham
Cove

Gordale
Scar

SETTLE

1

Malham

Burnsall

Appletreewick

Start

Simon's
Seat

Airton

Hetton

B 6160

Bardon
Tower

12

Bolton
Abbey

B 6265

A 65

A 65

SKIPTON

A 59

PROLOGUE

I ARRIVED at the foot of Malham Cove as the shock waves created by the last school party of the day died on the frosty air. An old man moved creakily off towards the village. I was left with a winsome robin – and a duck!

Rays from the westering sun tinted the normally bone-white cove, not with the usual reds and purples but with gold. The mallard drake, afloat on Malham Beck, "shot" rapids which had golden highlights. Elsewhere, the water was as "clear and cool" as when Charles Kingsley, cleric and novelist, was here, looking for water-babies to write about.

Kingsley described the fishing for trout at Malham Tarn as "the best in the whole earth". And just over the hill, in Littondale, returning to the water-baby theme, he pondered on the "stepped" limestone scenery and then arranged for Tom to jump from step to step while escaping from Grimes, his callous master:

"Then he went down three hundred feet of limestone terraces, one below the other, as straight as if a carpenter had ruled them... First, a little grass slope, covered with the prettiest flowers, rockrose and saxifrage, and thyme and basil... Then bump down a two foot step of limestone". And so on.

On the day that ended for me with a golden hue at Malham Cove, I had experienced the joy of walking the Malham Round by way of Janet's Foss, Gordale Scar, Water Sinks, Watlowes Valley and the Cove. The sun had the sky to itself. A light northerly wind sharpened the horizons.

I was solitary but never alone, having a strong feeling with every footfall that someone had been on the precise pieces of ground before me. It amused me to conjure up a few figures from the past – swarthy hunters from prehistory, monks and merchants, packmen and drovers, farmers and the first tourists, those gentlemen "of taste and leisure" to whom the Dales landscape was as little known as the upper reaches of the Amazon.

The story was updated by a modern shepherd, complete with light alloy crook, motor-trike and a dog as the pillion passenger. We nodded to each other but did not speak. There was nowt much to say. And off he went, in a fug of exhaust fumes.

Change is in the nature of things, whether it concerns the landscape or the people. In the ash-grey dusk, as I returned to Malham, I stopped at the roadside to watch two young men repairing a gap in a drystone wall. As they worked, the tinny strains of "pop" music emanated from a radio on their Land Rover, which was parked nearby.

I decided to extend the pleasures of a day in the limestone country by touring the Dales – not as a single spell of walking but whenever an opportunity arose during a single Northern springtime.

The pace would be somewhat Wainwrightish, with time to sit down and look around. My walking-by-instalment plan would involve some 90 miles in all, journeying against the "grain" of the countryside in order to stay in the upper reaches of the dales.

I would cross vacant wine-red moors, part of those huge tracts of little-known country that lie between the well-known dales. I would doubtless have to queue at the stiles on Ingleborough, our most popular peak, which is climbed by about 120,000 people a year. I would face sandwich-eating sheep and bullocks looking more ferocious than they are.

That spring, I sampled on foot our diverse Dales Country, with its wind-raked fells and flower fields, limestone pavements and gritstone crags. This being lambing time, the area reverberated with the bleating of sheep. The becks were in lusty voice.

No two days were alike. A hill-walk makes you aware of the transient nature of Dales weather, sunny periods alternating with showers. The folk I met augmented the daily weather forecasts with their own observations. On a morning of bright sunshine and clear air, a farmer remarked: "They said on t'wireless it was bahn to be dry, but yon sun's too glisky. It'll 'appen rain."

And rain it did.

1

LIMESTONE
COUNTRY

En route for Malham I visit a dew-pond, "bone" cave and the spoil heap of a calamine mine. At the Cove, I ponder on "caverns measureless to man". I hear stories about Walter Morrison, the Craven millionaire, and the remote community on Malham Moor of which he was a benign ruler.

I awoke in the early hours of a March day to hear curlews calling – not the bubbling trills of high pasture or salt marsh but contact calls, *cour-li, cour-li*, from birds flying high above North Ribblesdale, heading northwards with the spring.

When daylight came, and my walk began, I met one of my favourite Dales farmers, who was being mobbed by hungry yows because he was carrying a plastic bucket, which the sheep had been conditioned since lambhood to recognise as a source of nutritious food.

I commented to the farmer on the apparent tameness of sheep. In the old days, they were apt to run away if a stranger approached. Now they are more inclined to mob him. The farmer reached into his bucket and showed me a handful of food pellets with which he was supplementing their diet of wizened grasses and hay.

"It's these that mek 'em bold," he said. "They're that good to eat, you could tame lions wi' em!"

I mentioned hearing the curlews. He looked pleased, and remarked: "I reckon t'back o' winter's brokken when thou hears a curlew shout. Aye, t'weather can cod [deceive] a tewit, but a curlew 'ods back till things is warming up."

I did not like to remind him of the years when tewits had been sitting eggs in snowy fields and curlews stood dejectedly on the capstones of walls waiting for the thaw.

My walk began on one of those days when mild weather unlocks the Dales flavours. I could smell spring.

My way led through Settle market place and up Constitution Hill, where once the dust was raised by packhorse trains heading for the high road to Langcliffe.

Among Settle's many characters was Blackie-White, who lived on the Hill and was conspicuous because he had a Father Christmas-type beard. His nickname was derived from his twin occupations of sweeping chimneys one week and whitewashing buildings the next.

The road became a rough track, with loose stones. I headed clatteringly towards what Settle folk call the "banks". Quite soon, the town had receded to a Lilliputian size. From its market place flanked by 17th century buildings, it had expanded to take in a creamery of vast size sitting in an industrial estate with the unlovely name of Sowarth.

Settle and Giggleswick (just across the river) are in sweet-and-sour country, the sweetness being limestone and the sourness derived from millstone grit of the west. I settled for limestone, taking a diagonal path which would lead me to the top of Langcliffe Brow. In one of the mini-woods planted by Langcliffe Estate a green woodpecker welcomed a new day with a ringing laugh.

Giggleswick Scar, which keeps the north wind out of the streets of Settle, stood with a gaping quarry where vast quantities of pure white rock, part of the Great Scar Limestone, had been crushed and transported all over the land.

11

Here was I, a quarter of an hour into my walk, grieving for the loss of much good limestone and a drastic change to the appearance of a Scar which features in geological text books throughout the land because it is adjacent to a major fault.

It did prompt me to ponder on the nature of limestone – a sedimentary rock formed in remote times in a clear, tropical sea. The rock is formed of the remains of countless shells, sea lilies and pieces of coral which had lived over 300 million years ago.

The Carboniferous limestones were teased – folded, fractured – deep beneath the surface of the earth. Eventually, the process of erosion stripped away the strata overlying them. Into view came the Great Scar Limestone – a grand and apt title – which outcrops spectacularly in the Ingleborough and Malham districts.

Looking across the valley on to the man-made crater in the limestone scar, I was aware of the whiteness of limestone in the Settle area, whereas down in Bowland and in the bands of limestone in the Yoredale Series of rocks, at a higher level, the hue is a darkish grey.

Limestone is susceptible to solution by rainwater. Streams sink and reappear at a much lower elevation as springs. The hills are honeycombed with natural shafts and galleries formed by the relentless erosion of water via joints in the rock. Cave roofs hold displays of stalactites which have grown in perpetual darkness but are revealed as dazzlingly beautiful when the light fixed to the helmet of a potholer strikes them.

I left the fields for the tarmacadamed road, and soon afterwards left the road for a track heading towards Langcliffe Scar. I was still absorbed by the topic of limestone and, from the farming point of view, the vital necessity of keeping some water on the surface for the farm stock to drink.

I recalled a chat with Arthur Raistrick, the Dales antiquary who, when this subject arose, recited Jack and Jill, who went up the hill to fetch a pail of water. Why, said Arthur, did they go up rather than down? He suggested it was because they were visiting a dewpond, which is a saucer-like depression lined with clay which becomes filled with water that cannot soak away.

Fred Bullock, of Settle, told me of repairing dewponds above Langcliffe and of adding large flat stones so that if the cows stood in the water their sharp hooves would not damage the clay lining.

I walked on one of those showery days when, in limestone country, the sky tones are darker than those of the land. The sky was blue-black from a passing storm cloud but the Langcliffe scars were creamy-white; they were so bright they might have had an inner power source.

I took an ankle-ricking path up a scree to visit Victoria Cave. Pieces of limestone clinked underfoot. Jackdaws flew by, uttering a chorus of metallic cries.

At the head of the scree-slope, the cave appeared to view – its mouth vast and dark, as though the scar was yawning. Inside, the rocks were plastered with glacial clay which, when stirred by the human foot, took on the consistency of Yorkshire Pudding mixture. Caving is a mucky business.

The stalactites and stalagmites of Victoria Cave which, at the time of its re-discovery early last century had adorned the roof in "fantastic forms" and "as white as snow", had long since been plundered by covetous visitors.

Something of their beauty was to be appreciated one February day when, after days of keen frost, a north wind was blowing powdery snow into deep drifts along the side of the Scar. I walked waist-deep up the slope to Victoria Cave to see a glistening icicle display. Stones at the mouth of the cave, covered with snow which was then

Double rainbow over Settle.

Attermire Scars, near Settle.

smoothed by the wind, resembled a bed of mushrooms.

Victoria Cave has affinities with the tomb of Tutankhamen in that both held treasures which were lost to sight for centuries until a lucky chance led to their re-discovery.

When Michael Horner, an apprentice plumber, with some lads and dogs, visited the Scar in the springtime of 1838, all they knew was that it held holes known to be frequented by foxes. A dog was put into one of the holes and it was heard barking underground, the sound reverberating in a large space.

The lads widened the hole and Michael crawled into a cave, though without artificial light he could not explore it. His hands encountered a metal object which he removed as a souvenir. When he showed it to Joseph Jackson, his master, it was identified as a bronze fibula.

Jackson (the Howard Carter of this Yorkshire tale) worked secretly at the cave, removing bronze objects, brooches and a collection of Roman coins. In a letter to Charles Roach Smith, a London antiquary, he recalled that "the entrance [to the cave] was nearly filled up with rubbish and overgrown with nettles. After removing the obstruction, I was obliged to lie down at full length and get in . . .

"In some parts a stalagmitic crust has formed mixed with bones, broken pots, etc. It was on this crust I found the principal part of the coins, the other articles being mostly embedded or trodden in the clay . . . When we get through the clay, which is very deep and stiff, we generally find the rock covered with bones, all broken and presenting the appearance of having been gnawed".

The excavation of Victoria Cave (for such it was named by Jackson in honour of the Queen's Coronation) was formalised in 1866, when a Settle Cave Committee received support from the British Association. In the spring of 1870 they organised the first "dig" in an operation which would transform the diminutive Fox Holes into a vast hole.

The archaeologists dumped their material outside, providing a level area which has now grassed over to provide a ledge for picnic parties – or solo walkers with thermos tea to drink and butties to eat.

From my high vantage point I looked across a sheep-haunted landscape where there appeared to be as much outcropping stone as grass. Limestone scenery, with its chalk-white scars, dry valleys and "pavements", has a special kind of beauty.

Having ventured into Victoria Cave – but not into the short passages where disturbed clay is as tacky as Gloy – I pondered on what came to light during the Victoria Cave excavations. Here was an insight into early animal and human life in what is now the Dales Country.

The story began about 120,000 years ago. The Victorian excavators found two layers of cave earth with a thick layer of glacial clay between them. When it was deduced that the clay was of glacial origin, it could then be presumed that objects found below the clay were pre-Ice Age or at least an inter-glacial period, for the ice came and went on several occasions.

It was most certainly a warm period, for the bones of hippo and rhino were found, along with the remains of hyena, which may have accounted for the presence in the cave of the bones of larger beasts. The more recent deposits contained traces of cold-weather fauna – reindeer, red deer and bear among them.

Finally, scattered about on or near the surface of the cave deposits were objects from the sunset period of the Roman occupation – the so-called Romano-British times. The most attractive were dragonesque brooches. It is tempting to think that this cave had been used as a place of interment.

It did not need much effort to conjure up a mental picture of a man who worked in the traditions of that master plumber, Joseph Jackson. Tot Lord, of Settle, was a greengrocer who skipped work whenever possible to indulge his love of cave archaeology and sport (he once shot a "white goose" on the Ribble marshes which, let it be whispered, was a regal swan).

Tot was more like a gamekeeper than either a grocer or an archaeologist, being burly, red-faced, tweed-clad and carrying either a gun or a stick with a "dibber" at the end, all the better to demolish mole heaps on the scars in the hope of finding prehistoric flints displaced by the mole's digging.

Tot was the founder and custodian of the Pig Yard Club, which began when men with like interests gathered in a room down the Pig Yard [where cottage pigs were slaughtered] and discussed caves and all the "goodies" they might contain.

Jackson's finds having been dispersed among a number of museums, Tot based the Pig Yard Club museum – a private venture – on the Victoria Cave collection, which had been given to Giggleswick School and was lodged in the old premises near the church.

At the time I knew Tot well, he and his family were ensconced at Townhead, a stylish house which had been the home of Dr Edgar and his family. Here he assembled his treasures, keeping the valuable items in a locked area and umpteen years of "Country Life" stacked at the side of the main stairway.

Tot and I would sit under a verandah in a high-walled garden and cal [gossip]. This being Tot's home, the verandah was decked with an elephant's skull and other curios. The garden was somewhat tropical in the vigour and profusion of its plant life, a palm tree being among the species fighting for survival. There was nothing mundane about the world of Tot Lord.

At quiet times, or when he was not occupying his special seat at the local cinema, Tot unlocked the door to his museum and showed me his treasures. He had a relic of the Pig Yard Club days in a board featuring the coat of arms, on which was painted a rope ladder, pick and spade, human bone and gladiatorial sword and a Roman brooch. Overlooking all was the outline of a pig's head!

Tot would show me the magnificent skull of the great cave bear (he had the much smaller grizzly bear skull for comparison) and an exquisite reverse barbed harpoon, made of antler and used by Early Man (some labelled him Azilian) when fishing in tarns left by the melting ice.

He exhibited with pride the dragonesque brooches found in Victoria and Attermire Caves. He pointed to what he called "the bone of contention". The matter was contentious because at the time of his discovery, deep in Victoria Cave, no one had been quite sure if it was animal or human.

Tot would chuckle and relate how a human tooth was found in the lower cave-earth, where the hippo and rhino bones lay. There was wild enthusiasm among the excavators until Birkett of Anley admitted the tooth was his. It had worked loose and he pushed it into the cave deposits just for fun.

Tot was persuasive. When he was excavating a cave on Giggleswick Scars on a Sunday, he persuaded his wife to visit the workings with a traditional lunch, including Yorkshire puddings. Tot liked his home comforts, and Arthur Raistrick mentioned a "dig" on Malham Moor when Tot camped out in a small marquee. At night he slept in a "proper" bed, complete with a brass headpiece.

On leaving Victoria Cave, I strode towards Stockdale, en route for Malham. In the valley

Victoria Cave.

was a large damp patch – the Attermire [place of otters?] which gave its name to the range of limestone turrets and scars forming one of the most spectacular examples of limestone scenery, one small hill taking on the shape of a bell.

Stockdale is a name relating to an outlying cattle farm – the only farm in this little valley, which has a few "beefers" but specialises mainly in quality sheep of the Swaledale breed.

I was on the limestone side of a valley where the beck is on the line of a fault, and which runs over a lip of limestone as Scaleber Force, one of the beauty spots visited in the 1880s by a young Worcestershire conductor and composer called Edward Elgar (who was friendly with Dr Buck of Giggleswick).

Beyond Stockdale Beck rises Ryeloaf Hill, where I was once terrified in mist by a strange moaning sound. It turned out to be a newly-installed windmill providing power for a radio repeater station.

Stockdale is austere but beautiful. Trees are so scarce that one pair of carrion crows nested on a wall top and another pair chose a depression on the ground, lagging it with sheep's wool. Those who knew about it could not wait for the eggs to hatch in order to have the uncommon sight of seeing crows being fed at ground level. Alas, the eggs were washed out of the nest by torrential rain.

Then there was the astonishing incident of a magpie that landed on the handlebars of a cycle being ridden between Settle and Kirkby Malham. This pet magpie was taken to Stockdale Beck for its weekly bath. Spying a cyclist, as it circled to dry its wings, the fearless bird planed down to investigate and the most convenient landing place was on the handlebars. The cyclist almost fell off the bike with surprise.

The footpath led me beside the limestone and out across the now quiet hills between Stockdale and Malhamdale, under a big sky. This was curlew country, with the streaky-brown birds hanging in the air like feathered kites before planing earthwards, the curved beaks opening as they uttered a bubbling trill.

It seemed the last place on earth at which to find slagheaps, but on and around Pikedaw I found evidence of mining for calamine, which was needed in the making of brass. This process involved the use of zinc in the form of calcined calamine along with granular copper in varying proportions.

The quality of the brass depended greatly on the purity of the calamine. It was calcined at a building in Malham village which became known as the Calamine House. Much of the output went to the Cheadle Brass Company of Salford. It was stacked on horse-drawn carts which rumbled off down the dale to Gargrave. Here the calamine was put aboard barges on the Leeds and Liverpool Canal, which connected with other inland waterways, providing an economic form of transport for bulky products.

Malhamdale has what is perhaps the finest headpiece of any Yorkshire dale – a 240 ft high limestone cliff. I was rightly annoyed when a visitor inquired about "that big quarry over there"!

Add to this a mysterious canyon in which the cliffs overhang grandly at the top, plus a waterfall behind which the Queen of the Fairies has her home, and you have the makings of a tourist "honeypot", which is now the case, with about one million visitors a year sampling the delights of Malham Cove, Gordale Scar and Janet's Foss.

In the Romantic Period – mainly from 1760 to 1820 – gentlemen "of taste and leisure" sampled the scenery but did not walk very far. James Ward painted Gordale on a large scale for his patron, Lord Ribblesdale. Wordsworth thought that Gordale was like a lair in which young lions couch!

Malham Cove.

Victorian visitors usually hired a conveyance or a guide. Their successors in the railway age left the trains at Bell Busk and walked up to Malham at Easter or Whitsuntide, returning home with tales of a far country.

The writer of one of the first guide books (1886) mentioned the "toilsome walk over the hills" and the difficulty of finding Malham, "but a conveyance may be taken from Settle or Hellifield."

Half a century earlier, Frederick Montagu, "of Lincoln's Inn", employed a guide for the trip from Upper Wharfedale via Kilnsey Moor to Malham Tarn. In his book about the Dales, he insisted that a guide was vital, "more particularly as it often happens that a mist creates a difficulty even to a person well acquainted with the locality".

Walter Morrison (1836-1921) used to walk, though he was a millionaire and owned Malham Tarn House, which he referred to as "my mountain home". He is recalled as getting off the train at Settle, walking into a local grocer's to buy a leg of mutton and carrying that mutton over his shoulder as he stalked up Langcliffe Brow, heading for his mansion by the Tarn.

When he was not carrying mutton, he strode at a steady mile-eating pace with his hands behind his back. He stuck out his chest like a prize cockerel, rejoicing in the fresh air and exercise which had saved his life when he was a weakly child.

No one I met in a cafe at Malham, except the proprietor, had heard of Walter Morrison, whose sayings and deeds were once gleefully told all over the Craven district. And there was no one to nod in recognition when I mentioned dear old Mrs. Brown, of the Post Office, who made a rich fruit cake, which she sold to visitors, especially cyclists heading home to Colne or Nelson, but pausing at Malham to stave off "hunger knock" with a piece of Mrs Brown's extra-rich fruit cake.

I looked over the bridge at Malham Beck, hoping to see one of the water-babies which were common at the time when Charles Kingsley, the cleric and novelist, fished in the Tarn and walked in the grand limestone country. No water-baby has been reported, except in the pages of his children's book, since that first sighting by an imaginative story-teller.

My book began with a duck swimming on a gold-tinted beck at the base of Malham Cove. I returned to the vast white cliff in company with tourists and school parties who made up a colourful, chattering throng.

Tot Lord came to mind yet again as I recalled the Craven Pothole Club's efforts to find a cave system behind the cove. They followed a natural fissure for a while and then needed Tot's skill with explosives to force a passage.

He [and I quote from memory an item in the Club journal] clambered down into the hole, complaining about his rheumatism and sciatica. He lit the fuse – and leapt out like a spring rabbit, "in case there was any air in the packing". Incidentally, the hole was eventually classified as the deepest man-made pothole in the country.

A flight of broad steps led up beside the cove, giving easy ascent to the limestone pavement where the clints [bare rock] and grikes [fissures between the limestone blocks] form an arresting grey pattern. Each stone has been given a marble-like finish by the tourists' booted feet.

From the edge of the pavement, I saw climbers dangling on ropes and a grey-green valley receding to a misty distance. The valley was laced with drystone walls which were numerous near the village. On higher ground they formed the classic grid-iron pattern of the enclosure period, commanding the attention of visitors, especially Americans, who refer to "those cute stone fences".

A Pennine wall has a simple anatomy. Here are two walls in one, built side by side, tapering with increasing height. They are locked together by large stones called "throughs" and the void between the two sides is filled with small stuff. The wall is adorned by capstones, which "turn the weather".

The waller, going by rack o' t'eye [keen eyesight] prides himself on not picking up the same stone twice. A Malham waller told me: "Ivvery cobble's got its face; but it isn't any fool can find it". If a wall is gapped, the material to repair it is readily to hand.

I did not lack company as I made my way by Cawden Hill to Gordale Scar. To the Romantics of the late 18th and early 19th centuries − those gentlemen and a few ladies who were looking for the real world after the sterility of neo-classicism − the scenery was awesome, even "dreadful".

At Gordale, the beck leapt from an eyehole in rock and seethed over rock covered with tufa [a deposit of limestone which has been in solution]. Pieces of limestone clinked under my feet. Sable-plumed jackdaws [as the Victorians called them] gave their clattering cries. Thomas Gray (1769) "stay'd there (not without shuddering) a quarter of an hour and thought my trouble richly paid, for the impression will last for life".

He and other tourists wrote about the crag-going goats, which were valued by the farmers because the nannies dropped their kids early in the year and had a good milk flow by the time the sheep were parting with their lambs. There was nothing like some goat milk as a pick-me-up in bad weather for a lamb which had lost its mother.

The folk at Gordale Farm watched with mixed feelings the spring ritual of bringing down goats from the crags to the farms. "Ay, they tried to drive 'em with the wind so they couldn't smell t'billy goats!" I was told by an old lady who in her young days visited the her uncle and aunt at the farm.

Gordale is no collapsed cave, as some guide books insist. This was a gorge created by a furious rush of glacial meltwater in the closing stages of what is popularly known as the Ice Age. The erosion continues, much of it by frost. As I stood in Gordale, enjoying the spectacle of rock and water, a frost-weakened rock landed about 10 feet from where I was standing.

Mr Montagu − he who needed the guide for the journey from Wharfedale to Malham − plucked up courage to ascend Gordale's main waterfall. "My guide waded across the water at the shallowest part, and considerably above his knees, with all the unconcern imaginable. I asked him if he intended me to follow the same feat; − he only answered by pointing to the top of the rock in the extreme left of the torrent, and as nearly perpendicular as possible."

The guide announced that they must go up there. Montagu commented: "I never thought the word 'must' sounded so imperious, particularly from so juvenile a voice".

At Gordale and Janet's Foss, the character of the waterfall is created by a lagging of tufa, which to Adam Walker (1779) were porous petrifactions, "crumbly when dry, and pulpy when wet, and shaped a good deal like crooked knotty wood".

Tufa gives Janet's Foss its fan-like appearance. The waterfall lies in an attractive wooded ravine where the clattering cries of jackdaws are replaced by the caws of rooks nesting in the trees. The Janet of the title, Queen of the Fairies, lived in a cave behind the water. How she managed to keep her ballet dress dry and her gossamer wings uncrumpled is unknown.

I ate my sandwiches while sitting at the head of the fall and, on a quiet day, bending over to look through the flow of water, to where a dipper, the white-bibbed water sprite of the Yorkshire Dales, was walking on the stream bed, looking for larva food, while air bubbles on its well-oiled plumage gave the bird a silvern appearance.

Limestone pavement, above Malham Cove.

Janet's Foss, Malhamdale.

Morrison was in the habit of calling at Gordale farmhouse after he had set off some visitors to the Scar. He would slip into the farm kitchen for a chat with Thomas and Betsy Newhouse, who made a fuss of him and gave him tea and oatcake, which Betsy made on a "backstone" and hung up to dry on a rack raised to the ceiling. The drying oatcakes looked, to strangers, like a collection of wash leathers.

Thoughts of the shadowy grandeur of Gordale Scar persuaded me to take this route to the Tarn. In the upper gorge, the jackdaws and the day-trippers chattered. A flight of broad steps provided welcome assistance up to the level ground, where spring sunshine had brought a glint rather than a gleam to the outcropping limestone.

This was a district of sheep ranges, with grey crags and outcrops and low horizons. The sky seemed vast and a sufferer from agoraphobia would have been in torment. As a centrepiece to this austere beauty was bird-busy Malham Tarn, grey as gunmetal.

The Tarn, 153 acres of water lapping on a bed of impervious Silurian slate, overflows as the lively Malham Water, which takes the first opportunity – the crossing of the North Craven Fault – to go underground. The phenomenon of the vanishing beck has had a strong appeal to visitors. William Bray, an 18th century commentator, wrote that "at one corner [of the Tarn] it runs out in a small stream...which in a short space rushes in full current into a heap of loose stones, and is there lost".

The school teacher with a class of anoraked children having an outdoor geography lesson had little difficult in controlling them as they stood, dumb-founded at the disappearance of the beck. What had been a good flow of water seeped away. It would reappear at Aire Head, about half a mile below Malham village.

In the parish of Malham Moor, which covers about 20 square miles, most of the sweet limestone ground lies between the 1,000 ft and 1,500 ft contour lines. The highspots, Darnbrook Fell and Fountains Fell, have the stepped topography of the Yoredale Series and are capped by millstone grit.

For over half a century, this was paradise to Walter Morrison, who had the time and "brass" to enjoy it. He walked by day and in the evening he would sit at home, smoking a pipe and reading such a book as Mr Bray's "A Tour into Derbyshire and Yorkshire" (1783), which was one of his favourites.

Bray described the ride to Malham Tarn as "truly wild and romantic". Here nature sat in solitary grandeur on hills "which are lofty, green to the top, and rise in irregular heaps on all sides, in their primeval state of pasture, without the least appearance of a plough or habitation for many miles".

I had first to clear Malham Tarn, walking along the normally dusty white track, beside the scar and trees growing unhindered by sheep because they stand in circular walls which stop the animals from browsing.

At this stage, my walk became something of a battle with the wind and with Malham Moor's own special brand of horizontal rain. It was a relief to take cover in a new bird-watching hide by the tarn and look out on to a stretch of water which was now choppy and chilly, each wave fringed white with foam.

The Tarn is topped up by a calcareous stream which has a strong flow, having benefited from the Moor's average annual rainfall of 58 inches. A dull sky is the norm, with measurable amounts of rain occurring on an average of 220 days and snow lying on the hills for around 40 days a year.

The imaginative visitor can people this high, sparse upland with historical personages – with the proud Lamberts of Calton (one of whom, John, was Cromwell's second-in-command) and the Listers of Gisburn, whose patriotism in raising troops to help defend the country led to them becoming my Lords Ribblesdale.

It was during the Lister ownership that ground lying east of the Tarn was levelled and a shooting box built. Trees were planted and in 1780 the outlet of the Tarn was dammed to ensure that the level remained constant, being some 14 feet in its deepest place. The Listers had an agent for their estate and mining interests. They owned the Colliery on Fountains Fell which tapped seams of brittle coal.

James Morrison, of Basildon Park, Berkshire, bought the estate in 1852 and his son, Walter (1836-1921) inherited it on his 21st birthday. Morrison, a great traveller, astute businessman, philanthropist and naturalised Yorkshireman, remained a bachelor and, according to his neighbour, Geoffrey Dawson of Langcliffe Hall, "never seemed to notice or care for comforts".

Dawson, who became Editor of "The Times", wrote of Malham Tarn House as being "solid and substantial...with big rooms, big windows and a big outlook". When the House was badly damaged by fire in 1873, no time was lost in re-building and on the eastern side was added an Entrance Front and an Italianate bell-tower [the latter was dismantled about 1963].

Morrison was no snob, and he loved to hear the local dialect, as rendered by Alfred Ward, his principal gamekeeper. If a visiting angler was talking poshly and said "water", Morrison would remark: "Don't call it water; it's watter! Ask Alf, if you don't believe me". Once, feeling doleful, Morrison said to his keeper: "Ward, you're so lucky to have a family...You'll have somebody to leave your money to". Alfred Ward replied: "You can always leave your brass to me!" Morrison laughed about this for days afterwards.

To the Tarn, in the days of the Morrisons, came Charles Kingsley, who as an honorary canon of Middleham was familiar with the Dales. In July, 1858, he recorded in a letter: "My largest fish to-day [a cold North Wester] was 1½ lb, but with a real day I could kill 50 lb. Unfortunately, it wants all my big lake flies, which I, never expecting such a treat, left at home".

In a succeeding letter – one in which he described the fishing as "the best in the whole earth" – Kingsley mentioned he was now researching a book on The Pilgrimage of Grace. It was never completed, though Kingsley had high hopes for it and had promised that "wonderful Malham Tarn will come into the book and all around it".

Morrison was never known to turn down an application from someone who wished to fish for trout or perch. He did insist that all trout caught which weighed less than one pound should be returned to the water. He himself fished the Tarn only once and netted a quarter pound trout. Delighted at his success, he ignored his own rule and took the fish back to the House.

At Malham Tarn, until well after the 1914-18 war had shattered the social fabric of the nation, lived a distinctive community, the members of which were dependent on the estate. Morrison's agent had the grand-sounding name of John Whittingale Winskill. He was a natty dresser, wearing a good suit, a grey bowler and having a watch secured to his waistcoat with a gold chain. Winskill was, in his manner and speech, the epitome of the Old English Gentleman, and he did not rush to correct anyone who mistook him for Morrison.

When Morrison left his house in Cromwell Road, London, for his "mountain home" in Yorkshire, he followed the gentleman's custom of taking some of his staff with him. Mr and Mrs William Skirrow, butler and housekeeper, also moved north. Mrs Skirrow, a Settle girl, enjoyed this summer sojourn and she was just as keen as Miss Lodge, the resident house-keeper at Malham Tarn, to keep dust at bay.

Malham Bridge (Bruce Simpson).

Gordale Scar (Den Oldroyd).

Mrs Skirrow's spring-cleaning took place almost every day of the year and Miss Lodge gloried in her ability to keep a spick-and-span house. Before the Derby Brights coal was put into the scuttle in Mr Morrison's drawing room, each piece was washed and polished.

The aforementioned Alfred Ward, the gamekeeper, caused some distress to Morrison when he began to court Ellie Earnshaw, the cook at Tarn House. He proposed marriage to her and then informed Morrison of his desire to leave. He would also be taking Miss Earnshaw with him. Ward explained that his existing accommodation was not sufficient for a married man. When Morrison realised he might lose a gamekeeper and a cook, he quickly made available a cottage called Sandhills.

Robert Battersby, the coachman, met visitors to Malham Tarn House at Settle railway station. With his white beard, he had a superficial resemblance to Morrison and he, like Mr Winskill, was pleased when strangers thought he was the owner of the estate. Just before the 1914-18 war, Morrison bowed to the inevitable and bought a car.

Robert Battersby had a rapid transformation from coachman to chauffeur. At the age of 75, he drove horse and carriage down to Settle, collected a Fiat car, was taken round the town a few times by its supplier, Billy Slinger, and then he drove the car up the steep hill to the moor.

It was said that when he reached the point at Tarn House where, in the old days, the horses had to turn into the yard, he shouted: "Whooa, lass! Whooa!" The car did not stop. Travelling on, it crashed into a gatepost and one of the lamps was smashed.

Malham Tarn lacked a pub and a shop but it did have a School, established in 1872, and administered by a committee of seven who were elected annually in Easter Week. The teacher was able to stay at school during the week, occupying some upper rooms. It was sparse accommodation, one of them recalled. "One room held a little desk, a table and some chairs, plus an oil stove; and in another room stood a bed, wardrobe and dressing table".

Nature walks along the edge of the Tarn introduced the children to birds and flowers. Farm children took time off in haytime. In the 1930s, the teacher commuted to school from her home at a mooredge farm, using a pony.

The way from Malham Tarn to Tennant Gill was a well-trodden section of the Pennine Way, the 250 mile long path which connects Edale in Derbyshire with Kirk Yetholm in Scotland. The smell of "good muck" pervaded the district as farmers took advantage of dry conditions to demolish the "muck heaps" or empty the slurry tanks.

Tennant Gill, named after a family of that name and now part of the National Trust's extensive Malham Tarn Estate, is one of the ideal places for a farm, having a reliable source of fresh water. Here, the flow of water turns a novel turbine which generates electricity.

Among the farms to be found around the huge bulk of Fountains Fell is Capon Hall (known in early times as Cap-man-how and long since abbreviated in speech to Capna). In the heyday of cattle droving, it was sometimes known as Traders' Hill, and Edith Carr, the farmer's wife at Capna for many years, evoked in prose "the wiry Scottish drovers who passed Capna with their lean, lank, long-horned cattle, mangy and scraggy after the weeks of walking from the Borders and beyond, through the long miles of the Pennines . . ."

To Abraham Banks, one of the "old school" of Malham Moor farmers, Capna was the centre of the world. Being whisked off to Leeds Infirmary for an operation, he lay on the operating table and overheard a staff nurse say to a doctor: "What a queer old man; I wonder where he comes from". Abraham, not yet knocked out by the anaesthetic, sat up and said: "I'm Abraham Banks; I come from Capna, on Malham Moor. Surely you've heard of Capna!"

Darnbrook House occupies a site used by Norse settlers over 1,000 years ago. It was said of Darnbrook that each winter it could be so cold that the farmer grew an extra skin. In 1942, the farm was snowed up for 10 weeks. "Winter can make a start in the middle of October and carry on until nearly May. There's a late growth up here. We don't see much improvement till June", I was told.

2

OVER
FOUR PEAKS

On Fountains Fell, I find traces of a Colliery, including a unique coke oven. I listen to the soulful call of "the Pennine Whistler". While eating butties at "t'back o' Penyghent", I speculate about the meaning of the name. At Horton, a retired Settle-Carlisle signalman tells me a railway tale. I brave the heights of Ingleborough. The "clarty" state of Whernside takes the shine off my boots.

Tennant Gill, Fornagill, Thoragill, Stangill — these farmsteads which huddle on the lower slopes of Fountains Fell testify by having absorbed the term "gill" to the necessity of a reliable water supply.

The v-shaped ravines which carry water from the Fell are fascinating places, especially where the terrain is steep and they offer sanctuary to indigenous plants and trees. In spring, a large gill is an echo chamber for the song of the cock ring ouzel, freshly arrived from its wintering grounds in the Atlas Mountains of North Africa. Because of its clear, fluty song, the bird has been called "our northern nightingale".

These thoughts came to mind as I strode northwards from Malham Tarn, which was lapping on its slaty bed but with the gleaming white cliffs of Great Close Scar and its neighbours as a backdrop. For a time, I had the free-draining limestone underfoot but my objective was Tennant Gill, one of those farms crouching against the flanks of Fountains Fell. I knew this sprawling eminence from old to be a clarty [moist and tacky] hill.

Spring is tardy on the High Pennines. Long after it has flooded the dales, colouring up the cottage gardens and has brought a tinge of fresh green to the fields in the dale, it is still storming the heights.

I disturbed a small flock of lapwings, admiring the birds' tufty wings and jaunty head crests, and then I flushed some newly-arrived pipits which would soon spread out across the uplands. The meadow pipit may not be the most conspicuous of the Pennine birds but it is undoubtedly the most common and well distributed.

Craven has long been famous for its sheep walks. The flora is rich and diverse. On the limestone reaches of Malham Moor grow yellow mountain pansy, wild thyme and, in marshy places, the mealy primrose (*Primula farinosa*). I have also found that strange-looking plant known as moonwort.

The Moor reeks with sheep, but cattle have always played a major part in the economy. The Norse settlers of 1,000 years ago would keep stocky black cattle as well as sheep and this was most certainly the case in monastic times, when Fountains Abbey ranched them both.

In summer, shepherds would gather the sheep from the sprawling fell and drive them along what is now known as Mastiles Lane — a green lane, between walls, but then just a well-marked track linking up monastic possessions. The baa-ing host of sheep, arriving at the grange at Kilnsey, were washed to remove from their fleeces the grit and grime.

When they had time to dry off and fill their bellies with dale grass, they were clipped and the wool sent by ox-hauled wain across the Grassington Moors to the Abbey, where it was stored in the cellarium to await the arrival of wool merchants, some of them travelling from the Continent.

Life on Malham Moor and the fells of Fountains and Darnbrook may have been hard but surely it was peaceful when the monks had overall charge. There was, in fact, much fratching and, following the Dissolution, disputes about what had been Abbey land frequently had recourse to law. Such disputes give us an insight into the old days.

For example, Ralph Buck (aged 80) who lived at Darnbrook testified that he had known Fornagill (the land in question) for eight years before the Dissolution. He had seen cattle, horses, etc., brought from the Abbey. Warming to his tale, Ralph added a touch of romance. He had seen "the heardes [men] milk the Abbeis Kyne in the same ground lying their swords and bucklers besides them whilst they were milking".

The Cowperthwaites of Tennant Gill showed me the simple, efficient water-turbine which generates electricity at this remote farm. There followed a slog up Fountains Fell. Nowhere was the going severe but it was, indeed, clarty. That day Fountains Fell was still coping with recent downfalls of rain; the fell leaked water as if it was a wet sponge.

Pausing to look back, I saw the gleam of sunlight on Malham Tarn. After the pearl-white limestone, I felt melancholic on the extensive summit of Fountains Fell, with its slabs of millstone grit. The earth tones were dark, with much peat. The vegetation was tously, featuring ling, bilberry, cloudberry and moss.

If you find a pipe on Fountains Fell, it was probably the one lost by Wainwright, fell-walker extraordinary, who dropped it on November 19, 1966. Wainwright, in his "Pennine Way Companion", mentioned that on the short walk from Malham Tarn to Tennant Gill an "imperceptible but important" watershed is crossed.

The walker leaves behind the gathering grounds of the Aire and now enters an area where the becks flow to the Wharfe. "The Pennine Way impinges only slightly in the drainage area of the Wharfe, however, for immediately north of Fountains Fell, Ribble country is entered".

Wainwright had aptly described the top of the Fell as "gently undulating and very extensive". I passed some imposing "stone men" to reach an area where the voices of the moor birds included the hoarse crowing of the red grouse and the low, double call of the golden plover – the "Pennine whistler".

A plover, standing at the edge of a peat bank, looked in silhouette like a long-necked wine bottle, the small head resting on a neck which had been extended as the bird took in the sights round about. Here was a golden plover of the southern race, less boldly marked than its northern cousin, with its coal-black underparts and gold-and-black mantle. The bird moves quickly when there is an intruder; it advertises itself in order to distract attention from its nest.

At the edge of the tarn, a dunlin ran with mincing steps. This so-called "plover's page", a smaller bird, frequents the same haunts, though with a preferance for hilltops where there are peaty pools. The dunlin is confiding, being skilled at deflecting the interest of an intruder from the site of its nest. On calm days, the cock bird descends on motionless wings, uttering a rapid trill which rests as light as thistledown on the thin moorland air.

My map of Fountains Fell showed "Coal Pits (disused)" and "Shaft (dis)", as well as the cairns and piles of stone. On either side of the hill are miners' trods, that to the west being frequently referred to as the Coal Road. Tread warily on the wet and misty heights of Fountains Fell, for here are deep shafts, not all of them being fenced off.

When, early last century, Lord Ribblesdale owned the Malham Tarn Estate, his territorial interests extended to the summit of Fountains Fell, where pits and shafts were dug to exploit the coal seams. Arthur Raistrick recorded details of its opening in 1807, with the technical help of surveyors and miners from the Burnley coalfield – men who had been brought in to help with the mining of calamine.

The bell-pits were not more than 20 or 30 feet deep, so the coal could be wound up by hand. Deeper shafts were being excavated from 1810 and the men who sank a pit of "six fathom two feet" were paid 40s a fathom. Edward Watson received £17.2s for "banking and making the road to the new pit". When William Brotherton spent two days carting stone to the "new pit", presumably for the lining of the shaft, he was paid 10s for his efforts.

The coal was carted off to be used for processing the calamine which was mined near Malham.There would be other uses, such as a source of heat under the cauldron where sheep-salve was mixed or in the domestic grate, where Fountains Fell coal needed a good deal of heat, such as from a peat fire, to ignite it and, when burning, was noisy stuff, spluttering and spitting.

The substantial stone building with the low arched doorway – referred to by Wainwright as "the igloo" – was not built for housing sheep, as many suppose. Nor was it constructed for benighted hikers, who would have had to go inside on all-fours. This was a coke oven of a unique design, part of the colliery complex that is such an unexpected feature of the summit of Fountains Fell.

William Hunter, of Cowside, believed that the last field kiln to be used in the district, in Victoria's reign, was at his family farm, Cowside. The fuel was Fountains Fell coal.

It was but one of several collieries in the dale country. A famous Colliery existed on Tan Hill, above Swaledale. Lady Anne Clifford, when visiting her Edenvale castles, warmed her ageing bones beside a fire made of Tan Hill coal, which someone called "a burnable shale".

From the rim of Fountains Fell, I surveyed the "back o' Penyghent", noticing its impressive profile and the particularly thick layer of limestone (where purple saxifrage flowers towards the end of March). Rainscar Farm was like a model on a planner's table. The sunlight brought a responsible glint from the roof of a car parked near the ancient site of Ulfgill Cross.

Penyghent (which I prefer to present without the hyphens) is a British name (penno = hill) in an area where Norse and Old English names are predominant. The Norse includes Cam (ridge), Selside (the saetr or summering place among the willows), Sulber (from sol, meaning sunny) and Swarth Gill (the black gill). Derived from the Old English are Horton (dirty land) and Helwith (a reference to flagstone).

As for Penyghent, does "ghent" come from gwynt, meaning "hill of the winds" or from cant, a reference to a rim? Could this be the Hill of the Border Country? The name Ribble, for the river, is believed to refer to a boundary. At one time, the English-Scottish border embraced most of the area which is now the county of Cumbria.

"Hill of the Winds" is appropriate, though it also applies to Penyghent's famous neighbours, Ingleborough and Whernside. I once reached the summit of Penyghent a few minutes ahead of a middle-aged couple who were making their first visit. They stood in silent contemplation. Then the woman remarked: " Eh, Fred – wouldn't this make a good drying ground for clothes?"

From Fountains Fell, my eyes swept a district of low horizons and a big, empty sky. They traced the course of the Stainforth-Halton Gill road near the Giant's Grave and by Penyghent House, one of the big sheep farms of the Pennines. I saw the merest trace, beyond Littondale, of Horse Head Pass, across which the local parson travelled on a white horse when he had the spiritual supervision of Halton Gill chapel and Hubberholme.

There was time at Rainscar for a brief chat with Eric Coates, the farmer. Rainscar achieved

Coke oven, Fountains Fell.

Rainscar Farm and Penyghent.

Pinnacle Rock, Penyghent (Bill Pates).

national fame when the BBC produced a documentary film dealing with the annual routine on a big Pennine sheep farm – the dipping, lambing, clipping, spaining [separating yows from lambs] and the cross country trek to Bentham auction mart, where they went through the sale ring.

John Coates, Eric's father, was a dalesman of the old type who was brought up to handwork. I remember seeing him hand-raking hay in the brassy sunlight of a July evening. Another memory that came back to me as I strode from Fountains Fell via Rainscar to Penyghent was Herman Hemingway, bird photographer, struggling through snow drifts to a raven's nest and seeing the sitting bird – the only black object in a white landscape.

I looked in vain for what had been a familiar object by the metalled road at Dale Head and that was the base of Ulfkil Cross, one of the territorial markers of land owned by Fountains. I had last seen the hollowed-out block of stone in a tangle of vegetation near what used to be a gate and is now a cattle grid.

Having decided it could not have gone far, I looked over a wall and – there it was, well away from the road traffic. "Ulf" was a fairly common Norse name, found also in the Lake District. One of the Ulfs owned land in North Ribblesdale and Upper Wharfedale. His son gave property to the monks of Fountains in 1175.

The cross was raised at a time when there were no detailed maps of this area and hardly any walls. On the uplands, the boundaries were described in relation to natural features, especially ridge-tops and the course of becks, "where heaven's water descends". A cross such as that behind Penyghent would have the visual impact of an exclamation mark as well as sanctifying the area.

Ulfkil Cross, which stood on the watershed and at the point of convergence of several ancient routes, was a rallying point in 1536 for local supporters of the ill-fated Pilgrimage of Grace, a northern rising objecting to the Dissolution of the Monasteries. One of its supporters, Sir Stephen Hamerton, of Wigglesworth Hall, was arrested and examined.

He said he had first heard of the insurrection in Yorkshire "by a bill set on the Church door of Gyglesweke [Giggleswick] before the first commotion in Craven, summoning all to meet next morning at a place above Neales yng [Neals Ing]". Sir Stephen claimed that, having gone next morning to see the bill, he found the people had gone to the meeting place taking it with them. Another time, returning home after hunting, he was surrounded by 300 armed men who had forced him to take the oath.

Meanwhile, the Giggleswick Pilgrims met at the cross and sang a quaint hymn composed by a monk of Sawley. The Pilgrimage collapsed. For a time, the hangman was busy.

Impressed by the name of the Cross and its wild situation, Jack Rayner in 1975 devised The Ulfkil Stride, a 33 mile challenge walk over the fells, beginning and ending at Buckden. The course involves 5,000 feet of climbing over Horse Head Pass, Penyghent, Fountains Fell and Old Cote Moor.

So to Penyghent. From Dale Head, the Pennine Way swings to approach the "nose end" of the big hill, on a path with new, durable stretches to protect the landscape, which was being transformed by boot-power into a porridge-like mush of peat and clay.

I met walkers from Brackenbottom. One of them told me that the stile at the edge of the hamlet had proved to be a bottleneck, but soon the youngest and daftest Three Peakers were in rapid ascent of the foothills. They clumped along a board walk.

A skylark sang, a meadow pipit descended in "shuttlecock" display flight and, from some mossland, came the chittering of a snipe. I discussed boots with an elderly walker. He bought some eighteen months ago and had already travelled well over 1,000 miles.

I mentioned the recuperative properties of a hot bath. He told me that he added some "extract of horse chestnut" to the water.

My view of Penyghent changed. The hill lost its lion-like shape. I looked up a recently-created boulder slope just as a doleful West Yorkshireman shouted: "That's not all, lad. Tha can't see top 'alf from 'ere. Tha's nobbut just started".

I was overtaken by a dog which had a large stone in its mouth; it was setting an example to those whose carelessly-placed boots had led to fearful erosion and a cascade of stones down the slope.

At the summit of the hill, over 2,200 ft above sea level, I was greeted by a Dales-bred yow. The animal nuzzled my rucksack as I lowered it from my back on reaching the cairn. I once had a conversation on Penyghent with an elderly walker and it was a classic example of dales brevity. He said: "Three Peaks?" And I replied: "Yes". He inquired: "First time?" And I said: "No". There was a pause before he remarked: "Oh — you know what you're in for then!"

Now there was only a sheep to talk to, the others being Three Peakers — "straight-necked 'uns", who did not look left or right as they burnt up the miles.

John Wood, writing in "Mountain Trail", his most readable book about the Pennines, was somewhat critical of Penyghent: "My main criticism of the view from Pen-y-Ghent is that it does not include Pen-y-Ghent. Subject to this inevitable limitation it is worth seeing, though Whernside, Buckden Pike and the rest — even Ingleborough — are second-rate compared with the one on which we are standing. Besides, most of the southern landscape is blotted out by the broad bulk of Fountains Fell; and Plover Hill, the Siamese twin of Pen-y-Ghent, does the same for the north-east".

He would have liked it even less if the mine workings had still been active. Penyghent, like Fountains Fell, had its coal workings. William Howson (1850) recorded: "Near the summit are some horizontal shafts from which coal is procured for lime burning, and near the cart track below these, a scanty spring...may be found".

The western side of Penyghent, which I now descended, had been "loved to death" — lacerated by the boots of walkers. The battle to halt the erosion on the Three Peaks began in the early 1980s, being concentrated where areas of peaty ground had taken on the appearance of first-world war Flanders, being from ankle to knee deep in brown ooze which had the consistency of Yorkshire pudding mixture.

In 1986, the average path width was measured as 11.4 metres, or about twice the width of a B-class road. The Three Peaks Project was established in the following year and a number of techniques were tried to bind the footpath and restore the gravely damaged ground on either side.

The reinforcement of the surface of paths involved such varied materials as geo-textile mats, stone chippings and boardwalks, with stone being pitched on the old-fashioned way to control erosion on Ingleborough. Fertiliser stimulated growth on the reclaimed areas. It was all very unsightly but necessary.

Many moons have waxed and waned since I first "did" the Three Peaks with Ken Pounder. We had difficulty in finding the best route on an unlacerated landscape. We could not ask anyone the way because we were the only people walking it that day. I shuddered at the sight of Penyghent on my slithery descent to where some reinforced footpath stood out straight and white against the dun colours of the fell.

Modern technology has been used, and the Three Peaks invaded by mechanical monstrosities such as the helicopter which appeared clatteringly over Little Ingleborough

Nether Lodge, Ribblesdale.

Ingleborough from Scales Moor.

in the spring of 1990 with loads totalling 120 tonnes of fine-grained sandstone chippings for reinforcement of the path on this fell.

A few months later, a Unimog was spraying seed on Whernside. An area of 14,000 square metres — "equivalent to three and a half football pitches", said the project officer — was hydro-seeded, using a spray gun. The mixture consisted of ryegrass seed, fertiliser and soil. Within a month, the grass had begun to establish itself. It was assumed that in due course it would be replaced by native species spreading in from moorland areas round about.

Alas, poor Pennines! I now walked on ground that was little better than a scree slope. Three Peakers long since broke away from the recognised right of way between Penyghent and Ribblehead. The sign to Horton is ignored. Successive parties go directly ahead, ultimately through Black Dub Moss bog and Red Moss bog to the Promised landscape of the dalehead.

On that stretch, I once saw a middle-aged man fall into Hull Pot Beck and a young walker sink to his waist in cloying peat during what turned out to be a classic case of bog-hopping. I was overtaken by three young men who had one haversack. Each wore it for half an hour and then passed it to the next on the rota.

A bass-baritone sound among bird calls — *prruk, prruk, prruk* — directed me to a passing raven. A small number of ravens from the Northern Pennines winter on the Yorkshire stretches and nesting has taken place in the Three Peaks area.

Wordsworth, who was no stranger to the Dales, especially Malhamdale and Wensleydale, had an ornithologist's eye. He wrote about seeing a raven that was "not hovering like the kite, for that is not the habit of the bird, but passing onward with a straight-forward perseverance, and timing the motion of its wings to its own croaking". He added that "the iron tone of the raven's voice, which strikes upon the ear at all times as the more dolorous from its regularity, was in fine keeping with the wild scene..."

Almost all the Pennine raven nests are on crags. The nests are formed of substantial twigs taken from rowan or thorn trees, with the addition of heather and a lining of wool plucked from the corpses of sheep. Approaching too close to a raven's nest in my more acrobatic youth, I would watch a bird glide, soar, somersault, dive with partly-closed wings or bank to reveal its handsome profile and dangling legs. The ponderous black beak had silver highlights, mirroring the sun's brilliance.

Now and again, the bird would land heavily and, in its agitation, pull up tufts of coarse grass, tossing the pieces into the air, where they were windborne like fine confetti.

I left the main path to Horton to stand beside Hull Pot, a quarry-like hole created by the erosive force of water and innumerable rockfalls. Climbing into Hull Pot is extremely difficult without potholing tackle. It is also unnecessary for everything can be seen by a visitor who walks around the rim and looks down — taking care, of course, for a fall into the pothole would lead to something more serious than a headache. This being limestone country, the water takes a subterranean course to Brants Gill Head. The rift of Hunt Pot is most definitely for the experts.

Potholers — or, to use a posh name, speleologists — are a characterful lot. The century-old Yorkshire Ramblers' Club were pioneer potholers from the time when a Frenchman, Edouard Alfred Martel, popularised the exploration of limestone shafts and galleries by being the first man who (intentionally) set foot in the main chamber of Gaping Gill, some 340 feet below ground level, on the slopes of Ingleborough.

The Ramblers, using hempen ropes and rope ladders, dangled in potholes which had grand-sounding names like Rowten Pot and Boggart's Roaring Hole. Old journals of the Club and of others which were formed with the specific task of exploring the underworld, are full of dry humour.

In one account of an underground exploration, the author mentioned someone by name who jog-trotted across a large chamber "with a boulder half the size of Leeds Town Hall trundling slowly behind him". At Horton-in-Ribblesdale, I overheard a brief conversation between a local woman and some potholers who were overtaking her on their way to Penyghent. "Nay, lads," she remarked, "doesn't ta think tha'll spend enuff time below t'grund wi'out going there now?"

At Horton, I chatted with Peter Bayes of the *Penyghent Cafe*, who voluntarily keeps a record of the Three Peakers and awards a certificate to those who complete the circuit in less than 12 hours.

George Horner, retired railwayman, related the tale of a man who bought some meat from a butcher. When they met a few days later, the customer complained that the meat he bought was so tough he could have soled his boots with it. The butcher asked him why he didn't do it then. Said the customer: "Cos I couldn't drive t'nails through it!"

Horton, as the most popular starting point for the Three Peaks Walk has something of the colour and bustle of a frontier town on summer week-ends as people prepare to reach the summit cairns of Penyghent, Whernside and Ingleborough within 12 hours. (The young and lish go round the 25 mile circuit, climbing a total of 5,000 ft., in considerably less time than this).

On my way to the footpath for Ingleborough, I passed a field where tents had sprouted like colourful mushrooms. The car park was full, of course, and a line of parked vehicles stretched from the river bridge to the station approaches.

The first-known Three Peaks Walk took place in 1887. It had not been planned. Two teachers at Giggleswick School – J. R. Wynne-Edwards and D. R. Smith – decided after a busy spell in the classroom to climb Ingleborough, which they did, with energy to spare.

It was one of those sunny and warm days which seem to have no intention of ending. The two teachers were lured on to Whernside by the sight of the fell's whale-back form lying just across Chapel-le-Dale. And having attained the summit of Whernside, what was more natural than that they should return home via Penyghent?

Ten years later, members of the newly-formed Yorkshire Ramblers' Club, living up to its name, walked the Three Peaks circuit in 10½ hours. It became a source of Yorkshire pride to have "done" the Peaks in less than 12 hours. Soon, walkers were being overtaken by runners, who brought the time down to less than three hours.

Eventually, a foot race was being held in spring and a cyclo-cross in autumn. The cyclists, carrying their light alloy machines for a good deal of the way, were at an advantage on the rough tracks and the dale road. They travelled light, but needed to carry nourishing food to stave of "hunger knock" and its debilitating successor, known as "bonk". Most of the competitors take Mars bars but one man was "partial" to rice pudding patties.

I had no intention of breaking a record. At Horton station I crossed the line by a board walk and was soon walking through the meadows, not far from Beecroft Quarry, a gash in the limestone which must be visible from outer space. Here, too, was the jade lake, a hole which filled with water and has an attractive blue-green appearance.

When I had left the meadowland, my feet encountered a hard track between outcropping limestone. It was tempting to turn and survey the broad, shallow head of the dale, the drumlin field consisting of low rounded and grassed-over hills which had originally been

Horton in Ribblesdale (D. Dakeyne).

Brackenbottom, on a minor road near Horton-in-Ribblesdale (D. Dakeyne).

a mush of clay and stones left by the receding ice. Penyghent had taken on the appearance of a maned lion in recline.

I crossed tewit land [where lapwings nest], heading for Ingleborough, which was represented by a powder-blue form beyond the gleam of limestone. Sulber Nick, a strip of green between limestone pavements led me to the foot of the mountain and the track with an easy gradient which would take me directly to the summit plateau.

What had been a peaty path had been covered by a harder material which settled to form a durable crust. I was aware of space and the rounded forms of hills. A skylark sang. Otherwise I walked in quietness until I heard water flowing down a stone staircase towards Gaping Gill, one of Britain's largest underground systems. Fell Beck plunges into the main chamber from a lip of limestone and tumbles for 340 ft before hissing against a bank of shingle.

I have already mentioned the first descent of Gaping Gill by the Frenchman Martel in 1895. He went down alone. He had no idea what lay at the bottom. On his frail rope ladder he must have felt small as he looked around a chamber which is 500 ft long, 110 ft high and 90 ft wide. He was rather like a spider dangling at the end of a fine thread under the dome of St Paul's Cathedral.

The odd thing about Gaping Gill is its lack of legends and traditions. You would think that with a shaft that size there would be an account of a monster lurking in the depths. Apart from the general notion of the countryfolk that the potholes and caves through which water flowed at the time of the Great Flood, when Noah became an admiral, there is just the strange, improbable tale published in a periodical called "The Lamp" in 1892 [only three years before Martel's visit].

This tells of a man who fell down, miraculously survived and encountered another man who told him he had fallen down two years before and had since been living off fish he caught in the underground stream!

Martel descended with a lantern fashioned on his arm and a package containing candles, magnesium and a flask of rum, sealed with watertight wax cloth and fastened to a wooden bar on which the Frenchman sat. It took him 23 minutes to descend and 28 minutes to climb back. Blue with cold and desperately in need of food and hot drink, he was applauded by the hundred or so people who had assembled at the head of the shaft.

I knew one of them, W. K. Mattinson, and I was in a small party of naturalists from Austwick who descended, one by one, sitting in a bosun's chair operated by a petrol-driven winch. In that same party were Mattinson's daughter and a grandson. When I mentioned this to one of the potholers on duty down below he said: "I suppose the next one down will be the ghost of Martel!"

In 1907, the Ramblers who went down by rope ladder had the company of Reginald Farrer, of Ingleborough Hall. Reginald had made a name for himself as a writer, artist and plant-collector. His prose had a fine style, as evidenced by his description of Gaping Gill's main chamber:

"The Great Hall…must be the original dwelling of Aiolos. For all the winds are at home here, and a hundred conflicting eager draughts welcome one to the Underworld. And a dim, awful world it is. Feet and yards give no impression, when numbered by hundreds.

"But this cave is terrifyingly vast – so high and so broad and so long. Almost in the middle, pale and ghastly, falls the daylight, in one round blotch of greyness. And through the daylight, in an avalanche, falls the crashing whiteness of the waterfall which, long before it touches earth, breaks like the Staubbach [a Swiss waterfall] into a never-resting cloud of spume…"

Looking back into the main chamber before he explored one of the passages, Farrer compared the sight with "some midnight view of a vast cathedral wrecked and pillaged, with pale moonbeams falling through a great rent in the dome".

A surge of energy brought me to the 16-acre triangular plateau of Ingleborough (2,372 ft). Here were the sparse remains of an Iron Age hillfort, being faint traces of horseshoe-shaped huts and a drystone wall extending round the plateau. A heap of stones was all that remained of the castellated tower built at the instructions of Mr. Hornby Roughsedge, when last century he became Lord of the Manor of Ingleton.

This tower or "hospice" was partly destroyed on the day it was officially opened. Some of the workmen, being "the worst for drink" – as Victorian temperance workers used to say – began pulling down the tower. Roughsedge left the hill in disgust. All that remains is an old sketch of the tower showing the damage – and the heap of stones, some of them – alas – having been taken from the old hill fort.

A tractor and trailer reached the summit of Ingleborough in the year the present Queen was crowned. Local men used this means of transport for the cement and other materials needed to make the windbreak, which was built in her honour. A mountain-indicator occupies the central position of the windbreak.

Just before the indicator had been put into position I reached the head of Ingleborough to see "something" wafting in the breeze. It turned out to be an aspidistra, with a note said to be from Gracie Fields, the entertainer who frequently sang about the "biggest aspidistra". The note claimed for the Ingleborough plant that it was the "highest" in the land.

John Hutton, a parson, in his tour of the caves published in 1781, summed up the feelings of many who climb Ingleborough when he wrote of taking "many a weary and slippery step", though he and his companions were "amply repaid when we got to the top, with the amusement we received in viewing the several extensive and diversified prospects..." That view takes in the wild fells of the Pennines, Pendle Hill, the gleam of sunlight on the wet sands of Morecambe Bay and the mountains of Lakeland, huddled on the northern horizon, steep and smooth, like an encampment of grey tents.

A steep slope, recently laid with stones, to provide a rough staircase, was my course off Ingleborough. I lost height at an exciting rate and then had the elation of striding along a boardwalk. Sections of boarding, with hinges to provide a connection, offered a narrow but firm way across a peatscape which in the past was a landscape on which to flounder.

The boardwalk, condemned as an unwelcome intrusion by some, does conserve the landscape, which in summer is whitened over, as with snow, by the downy fruiting heads of cotton grass. More "rural furniture" was seen in the wooden stiles spanning a wall between the nature reserve of High Lot and that of Southerscales, which is managed by the Yorkshire Wildlife Trust.

I was at the level of limestone, where extensive pavements look sterile but hold within their grikes [fissures between the blocks of limestone] the remnants of a diverse woodland flora. The path lay beside Braithwaite Wife Hole, the largest shakehole in Yorkshire. The funnel-like crater usually contains a pair of ring ouzels, the fluty song of the cock bird having a special quality in such an echo-chamber as this.

Southerscales, where men have farmed the ground since prehistory, was a typical Dales farm on which the land was managed as part of a traditional stock-keeping routine. Now that this land was bought for a nature reserve, botanists have studied the interplay of traditional farming with the natural scene.

Having made the area stockproof once again, they have re-introduced the traditional

Ingleborough from above Kingsdale (P. Gordon).

Limestone formations in a Yorkshire cave.

grazing regime of cattle in summer and sheep in winter. The sheep are hand-fed (when necessary) in the Fell Paddock, using hay made from the grass of local meadows. No chemicals are used on the reserve.

Parson Hutton, who huffed and puffed his way to the top of Ingleborough in the latter part of the 18th century, was astonished at the bleakness of Chapel-le-Dale and quoted from the poet Butler:

A Jesuit never took in hand
To plant a church in barren land.

Hutton observed that the chapelry "produceth neither white, oats, barley, peas, or any other sorts of grain; nor apples, pears, plumbs, cherries, or any kind of fruit. A ripe goose-berry was a natural curiosity in the summer season, in most parts of the district; even their potatoes they have from other places".

The dalesfolk might lack those products, but they were blessed with others equally valuable, "excellent hay grounds and pastures" plus "large flocks and herds of cattle, which enabled them to purchase every conveniency of life". Living detached from "the luxurious, vicious and designing part of mankind, they were temperate, substantial, sincere and hospitable".

Hutton and his friends, meeting the local curate, were reminded of lines from Goldsmith:

A man he is to all the country dear,
And passing rich with thirty pounds a year.

After becoming a little nostalgic for the *Hill Inn* of the Kilburn family — their guests included Edith Summerskill, Geoffrey Winthrop Young and Lord Tweedsmuir — I refreshed myself at what is now the *Old Hill Inn* and strode off towards Whernside, the largest but my least favourite of the Three Peaks.

The chief advantage of being on this long bare ridge is that it offers splendid views of those other Peaks and also overlooks Ribblehead viaduct on the Settle-Carlisle Railway. It also has a superb drystone wall which runs for a mile or two from just above the Ingleton Glens to the highest point at 2,414 ft.

I climbed Whernside from Bruntscar, one of the string of little farms of Norse origin lying along the edge of the fell, each backed by limestone scars and each having a spring close by.

Towards the end of the climb I encountered the effects of erosion, not just primary erosion but damage to a flight of steps, presumably installed to conserve the ground. The steps had degenerated into almost useless bits of wood. Not surprisingly, visitors were creating more erosion in their attempts to by-pass them. Whernside, like the other Peaks, is being "loved to death".

I trudged along the breezy ridge, stood beside the trig. point, listened to the golden plover's sad whistle and descended towards Ribblehead through areas of and churned-up peat and mud. The path lay near Force Gill, where a waterfall leaps from a lip of rock, and across an aqueduct carrying the beck over the railway.

3

HEAD OF
RIBBLESDALE

I have a bad attack of Settle-Carlitis and recall some tales of Blea Moor. I visit a "shanty town" beside Ribblehead Viaduct and then climb to a platform underneath the arches. At Gearstones, I ponder on the 18th century sales of Scottish beef cattle and one of the minor exploits of Young Mr. Sharland, a Tasmanian railway engineer.

It was not by chance that my arrival at Ribblehead coincided with that of the "Flying Scotsman". As my old friend Bob Swallow says: "You've got to get your priorities right." My day's walking had been well-planned, even allowing for the fact that almost all the "steam specials" on the line run about half an hour late.

Some great locomotives — "Sir Lamiel", "Duchess of Hamilton" and "Bahamas" — have raised steam and great expectations when storming The Long Drag, as the first 20 miles of the Settle-Carlisle railway are collectively known.

An hour before a steam-hauled train is due, the enthusiasts muster with cameras and sound-recorders. At the appointed time, the sun shines, the wind is moderate, fingers twitch as they hover around shutter-release buttons and all seems well with the world.

Half an hour, or even an hour later, a plume of white smoke announces the train's delayed approach. Sod's Law has been at work. The "perfect conditions" have gone, to be replaced by the typical Settle-Carlisle "mix" of mist and rain.

In the days of working steam, a gale from the west prompted the footplate men to cower behind whatever shelter they could find in the cab and let the train drive itself across the viaduct. A workman on foot did at least have protection from the parapet on the weather-side.

There was time, before the arrival of "The Flying Scotsman", to follow the old railway track up Blea Moor to the heaps of stones which had been painstakingly raised up the shafts from the heart of the hill. I looked out over Dentdale, then returned to the signal box and to what remains of a small group of dwellings erected to accommodate what the Midland Railway loftily called "railway servants", in this case the maintenance men employed on a length taking in the tunnel and viaduct.

Blea Moor tunnel was driven through gritstone, shale and limestone. For the first 350 yards (from the south) it curves. Then it straightens out for the rest of the 2,629 yards, reaching a depth of 500 feet below the moor top. The tunnel is faintly illuminated in three places by daylight filtering down the ventilation shafts. Apart from the recesses into which workman can step if a train is approaching, the tunnel boasts a Donkey Hole about which nothing reliable is known.

Blea Moor itself would be a dreary place but for the presence of the railway. Until the coming of the Settle-Carlisle, a ghost — Lile Hob — enlivened the place. Hob was not a fearsome type of sprite. He was lazy, sneaking lifts on carts passing along the old turnpike. He has not been seen for years.

To read accounts of the construction period is to be charmed by the phraseology and fascinated by engineering detail. In 1873, when the tunnel was "in a great state of forward-ness", a correspondent of "The Lancaster Guardian" jotted down his impressions of the work, noting:

Blea Moor signal box.

Salt Lake Cottages, Ribblesdale.

"No person can walk in the tunnel for an hour or more and listen to the thundering reports and reverberations of blasting, see the miners wielding with terrible force their sledge-hammers when drilling the hard rock, and breathe the thick smoke of the exploded dynamite, without feeling sympathy for those employed in such mining operations, and of seeing what a privilege it is to travel by rail at the rate of a penny per mile."

William Davison was one of the "tunnel gang" who worked by the light of a naptha lamp. Artificial lighting was useless on a day when up to 100 trains a day used the tunnel. When the smoke was slow to clear, it became so thick that a workman had to find his way along the tunnel by tapping a rail with a stick.

Mr. Davison was a Methodist local preacher who, when planned to take a service at Dent, carried his bike through Blea Moor tunnel so that at the other side he could free-wheel down to the chapel. The return journey demanded more effort. It was said of one local preacher that he rode his bike into a headwind and prayed to the Lord that the wind would change direction. It did – and he had a headwind on his homeward way!

A woman who spent much of her girlhood at Blea Moor, where her father was the ganger, recalled that the signal box was a major attraction to the children. One hot day in summer, she and her sisters looked after the box while the signalman went for a swim in the raised water tank.

Father used to clean the chimney at the house by tossing a railway detonator on to the fire. When a chemical toilet was introduced, he said: "Let them 'at uses it, clean it" and he vanished in the direction of his favourite pothole on the fell!

By the time I reached the vicinity of the signal box, I was in the grip of Settle-Carlitis, an incurable disease afflicting those who have fallen under the spell of the railway – this fast, all-weather route which, using the north-south valleys of the Ribble and Eden, with a "mountain bit" in between, connects Settle with the Border City.

Sufferers from Settle-Carlitis do not want to be cured. The complaint is alleviated when they return to the trackside to photograph a "steam special", as on this occasion, when the "Scotsman" duly passed, causing wild excitement among the assembled fans. Twenty minutes later, after a southbound diesel dispersed the smoke that had hung about the tunnel and shafts, Blea Moor lived up to its nickname of Smoky Mountain.

I walked beside the signal box, which has withstood a battering from the weather. I looked over the battered fence to where a clump of rhubarb had defied wind and frost in what used to be a garden.

Seeing a sheep grazing at the lineside, I recalled a story told to me by George Horner, of a sheep which lay in the four-foot of the railway when a fast train was due. A visiting inspector suggested that George might drive the sheep from the line.

George said: "Let her stop theer."

The inspector retorted: "She'll get run over."

George replied: "That's her look-out." He was not being callous, knowing that Blea Moor sheep are adroit and unflappable.

The sheep lay chewing her cud when the night express was offered. George recalled: "I got it on line and pulled off [the signal]. That inspector was keeping his eye on the sheep. In a bit there was a rumbling and t'express comes under t'bridge. The old sheep hadn't budged. T'inspector turned away; he said he could not bear to watch it."

The sheep stood up, stretched and walked out of the way of the train. "Yon express shot by her at about 60 miles an hour. The old sheep went back to that lovely dry trackbed and lay down again."

Steam special on the Settle-Carlisle railway at Stainforth, just north of Settle.

Ribblehead viaduct.

Dusk at Ribblehead has a special quality when the stories of the construction days are known, for it is then that the ghosts of navvies, their wives and children, stir in the areas where the shanty towns stood – towns with vivid names, including Batty Green, Sebastopol, Inkermann, Jericho, Jerusalem. When a shift ended, some men went to their homes and others converged on the "Welcome Home" inn for some hard drinking.

On the evening of my Peaks walk, I had the special pleasure of being allowed to walk on the scaffolding with which several piers were enmeshed during a £3 million restoration of this immense structure, which is about a quarter of a mile long, attains a maximum height of 105 ft and, with 24 lofty arches, provides Chapel-le-Dale and North Ribblesdale with a spectacular headpiece.

The resident engineer welcomed me to his office, where I saw the cores of dark limestone and of brick made from local clay and shale. These had been put in place on the viaduct 120 years ago. The bricks made at Ribblehead did not prove satisfactory when exposed to the weather, and especially the freeze-thaw conditions of winter. They were replaced by Staffordshire blues or Accrington reds.

I met some of the scaffolders in their cabin, where two beds had been made out of – yes, scaffolding and boards. This "shanty town" consisted of Portacabins and Portaloos. I was provided with a white helmet and given a conducted tour of the viaduct, climbing ladders, passing men who were drilling, or pumping grout into the piers or preparing them for pointing using a pressure system.

And high up, under the arches, at a time when the lights were being switched on and small birds were arriving to roost, I saw brickies from Cheshire performing the delicate task of filling cracks with new bricks, contriving with special equipment to hold them in place until the cement had set.

The sun was also setting! It went down as a red orb between Ingleborough and Twistleton Scars.

My walk was resumed next day. The road from Ribblehead towards Hawes reverberated with quarry traffic, which did not seem to upset the cock lapwings. They were diplaying in flight over the unenclosed moor.

Gearstones is a cluster of houses beside the old Lancaster-Richmond turnpike. There's a farmstead and a Victorian shooting lodge which, presumably, is on the site of an inn and is now used by visiting school parties. A building across the road was pulled down but the roadside trough, made of slabs of Helwith Bridge blue flag, remains.

Almost all the farms beside such a lonely road provided hospitality for visitors and some were inns. The Gearstones hostelry was particularly well-known, being in a strategic position near the junction of Ribblesdale with Chapel-le-Dale and Widdale.

Towards the end of the 18th century, it was visited by the Hon. John Byng, later Lord Torrington. He was travelling through the Dales on horseback. To Genial John, this was a sodden, misty area and Gearstones inn "the seat of misery in a desert".

A fair at which cattle of Scottish origin were on sale "added to the horror of the curious scenery". Beasts driven on the hoof from the far north were now surrounded by drovers, buyers and sellers, many of whom wore plaids. Cattle men thronged the inn and the edge of the moor.

Byng found there was no hay for his horse in the stable. At dinner, he was served boiled slices of stale pork and fried eggs, "with some wretched beer to which my hunger was not equal, and from which my delicacy revolted."

A visitor in the 1860s was John Sharland, a young Tasmanian engineer who was involved in surveying the route of the Settle-Carlisle line. It is said that when he and his men lodged at Gearstones, an overnight blizzard heaped snow against the building and they had to excavate a way through a drift to reach a drinking trough in the yard. I like to think the story is true.

Walter White, an observant Londoner who suffered from wanderlust, toured the Dales in the mid-19th century. He was forced to take shelter at the inn by "a swift, horizontal rain... laborious to walk against." On his way, he had seen a novel mode of bill-sticking. The bills, advertising "gimmer hogs for sale" was attached "to the sharp spines of tall thistles by the wayside."

White stayed at "the lonesome public house at Newby Head" which was "a modest house, a resort for cattle-dealers from Scotland, and headquarters for shepherds and labourers."

The fare was better than the lodging. He was provided with "three kinds of cakes, eggs, and small pies of preserved bilberries." Clean sheets lay on the bed but he also detected "a musty smell of damp straw."

4

THE DEVIL'S HIGHWAY

I tip-toe between the drumlins to Nether Lodge, a grand meeting place of footpaths, and then go a solitary way over Cam End. Memories of Cam Houses draw me back to this remote group of buildings near the headwaters of the Wharfe. At Greenfield Forest, I watch a dawn display provided by black grouse.

Gayle Beck, affected by some weeks of dry weather, had done its disappearing act. Rounded boulders marking the bed of the stream were snuff-dry. I could cross wherever I wished. A pair of oystercatchers, newly arrived for nesting, stood beside what used to be a beck. If wild birds are capable of contemplation, they must have been wondering when the water would return.

Oystercatchers are dandies, smartly attired in black and white, with long bills like sticks of sealing wax and pinkish legs. They are extremely noisy if their nest is threatened. Once, when I came across a nest with some newly-hatched young, an enraged parent bird dived at me and fluttered near my head.

In the soggy wilderness between the road and Cam End, the Ribble Way reaches an indeterminate conclusion. At least, I am never quite sure which spring is taken to be the source, possibly because I prefer to think that the source is not on the highest but the longest tributary, which would be Gayle Beck, which flows from the side of Wold Fell.

I visited the area some years ago, by permission of the farmer. It was fun to straddle the beck and think of the mighty outlet of the Ribble near Preston.

Wold Fell, which has some outstanding limestone pavements and is a glorious vantage point for Ingleborough, also sends water down Widdale to join the Ure, Ouse, Humber and North Sea.

I sat at the edge of the moor at Gearstones and pondered on the route I should take to Cam End. I might continue on the road towards Newby Head and cross the beck near a shooting "hut", finding the Devil's Highway, a romantic name for the course of the old Roman road.

Then I considered the route via Nether Lodge, which would spare me some road work. This, I decided, was the way for me, especially as it would begin with a crossing of my favourite packhorse bridge – a stone arch, like a rainbow set in stone, extending across Thorn's Gill.

The bridge needs attention. Meanwhile, it has some metal splints. But the simple stone arch endures after several centuries. Standing here, I looked down to where Gayle Beck, using the abrasive properties of small stones, had worn away the limestone in the form of circular holes.

There is no official right of way up the side of Thorns Gill. John Hutton, who came this way about 1781, would not see a single "no trespass" sign. He was a parson from the Kendal district with a fascination for what became known as geology. He was in this district, with friends, to tour the celebrated limestone caves.

They refreshed themselves at the inn and left their horses there as they explored a "subterranean wonder of nature called Catknot-hole." Before they were "out of sight of

Birds of the Yorkshire Dales
red grouse (above) *and the short-eared owl* (Frederick Watson; P. Allis)

day" they were "obliged to wade up to the mid-leg a few yards, through a little pool made by the rill, that comes out of this cave. The passage grew narrower, but wide enough to walk along with ease, except in one or two places, where we were in danger of daubing our cloaths [sic] with a red slime."

When the cave was constricted, Hutton and Co jibbed. "Perhaps if we had mustered humility and fortitude enough, to have crouched and crawled a little, we might have come to where the roof again would have been as high as we should have desired... The rocks jutted out, and were pendent in every grotesque and fantastic shape; most of them were covered over with a fine coating of spar, that looked like alabaster, while icicles of various shapes and colours were pendent from the roof."

Hutton was under the impression that Gayle Beck was the Ribble. He commented on its romantic cascades, pools and precipices, which were "not unworthy of the notice of a stranger."

My route lay across the gill to the ruined farmstead of Thorns, thence across an area of faint tracks and oozing water between the smooth, rounded forms of a large drumlin field, consisting of debris left by the local glacier. The bogginess of the terrain made it ideal country for birds of the wader family — curlew, lapwing, redshank. I also flushed one or two snipe.

The track led me to Nether Lodge, the Piccadilly Circus of the Pennines, being the meeting place of several important tracks, including the Three Peaks Walk and the Ribble Way. My object being to cross Cam End, I joined the Pennine Way and headed northwards.

Two tracks, one from Gearstones, the other from Horton-in-Ribblesdale, manage to find each other on a shoulder of the fell, at an elevation of 1,500 ft. The map shows "Roman Road" (from Bainbridge to the Lune Valley). The route would have been used in much earlier times.

In the 18th century, which is recent in historical terms, what became known as Cam High Road was part of the Lancaster-Richmond turnpike. In 1795, good sense and a healthy regard for winter weather on the High Pennines, led to the turnpike being re-routed through Hawes and Widdale.

John Byng, who we last heard of eating indifferent food at *Gearstones Inn*, wrote that if the local roads were bad, the country barren and the winters long, yet there were compensations for the local people. They had "plenty of coal, the trout fishing, and the grouse shooting; which is a season ardently wish'd for; and brings a short harvest to the small inns."

Byng found the Cam road fatiguing and tedious. When travellers began to take the "low road", the old hilltop route went into decline, so that by 1864 one William Dobson reported that the way over Cam was "now grass grown, and is seldom traversed, except by sheep and the shepherds on their way to and from the neighbouring hills, a better route from Horton to Geerstones having been found on the opposite side of the river." J. Radford Thomson (1878) wrote about "the old, disused high road... over Cam Fell to Hawes."

I left the Pennine Way to visit Cam Houses, a cluster of farmsteads occupying a wild situation to the south of Dodd Fell and overlooking the large conifer forest called Greenfield.

When the Lambert brothers lived there, Bob used to make a weekly pilgrimage to Hawes, theoretically on business, though he was soon indulging himself in good ale. One market day, when he had run out of money and was still thirsty, he saw a man trying to sell Model T Fords. Suspecting that if he showed interest, he would be invited to have a drink of something strong, Bob said he would buy a car if the man could deliver it to the farmhouse.

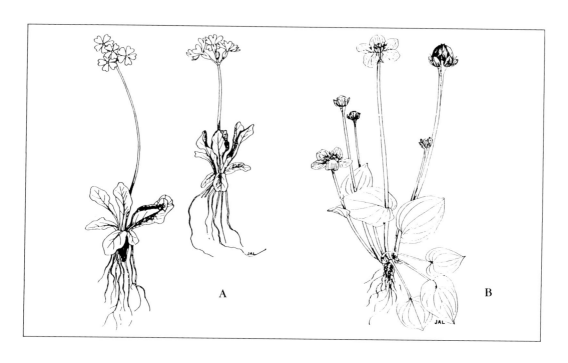

Flowers of the Dales – A. Grass of Parnassus; B. Bird's Eye Primrose (Joanna Langhorne).

Farm house in Widdale, between Ribblehead and Hawes (Ian Appleyard).

The dealer agreed. Bob got his ale. Next day the Ford Model T was driven towards Cam Houses – up the hill from Gayle [a name meaning "ravine"] and along a rough track to an expanse of soft fellside, where the vehicle sank to its axles, was dragged out and taken back to Hawes.

Kit Calvert, of Hawes, remembered the rough old way to Cam Houses. In the 1920s, when he was a young man, he worked at a farm in Wensleydale. The farmer asked him to drive some sheep from Bainbridge to Cam Houses, and Bob would meet him "on the tops" and indicate the allotment in which the sheep should be left.

Kit met Bob as arranged and was told that when he had dealt with the sheep he should go on to the farmhouse, where Eric Lambert offered Kit "a bit o' dinner". There were some snags. Bob had forgotten to buy "a bit o' beef" at Hawes, so they had eaten a "bit o' bacon" instead. The hens had not laid eggs recently, so all Eric could offer was "bannock and cheese".

The intended purchaser of "owd Scotch tups" reached Cam Houses to find them waiting in the parlour of the house for his inspection. In the 1930s, a time of economic hardship in the Dales, Kit Calvert and a friend went to Cam Houses to collect a white cow. They arrived just after a pig had been killed, an event celebrated by the purchase of a gallon of gin, about a quarter of which remained.

The visitors were invited to drink some tea with "cream" [neat gin]. Kit and Bob haggled over the price for the white cow and Bob eventually accepted the slightly lower figure if the visitors would play dominoes for "a penny a pop". This gave Bob a chance to recoup the shortfall on the cow.

To "cap it all", as they say in the Dales, the white cow slipped its halter as it was being led away. It wandered off – into a blizzard. The two men had to return to look for it on the following morning.

I first visited Cam Houses in the 1950s, when the approach was difficult for anyone with a wheeled vehicle. A tin hut called The Garage stood on the hillside and was being used as as hay store. A black heap [coal] and a white heap [lime] were moved to the farms by horse and cart as required.

A contemporary newspaper account mentioned that "no motor vehicle dare take a load further because of the absence of a road; in fact, the last stage of the journey is risky even for a pedestrian owing to the presence of bogs and swamps." And, the writer added, the souls at Cam Houses were brave to live "in the splendid isolation of moors and fells, 1,700 ft above sea level … where the dogs do not bark at the occasional stranger who comes that way but regards him with curiosity."

The youngest children of the Kitchings attended Buckden School, involving a seven-mile round journey. The kids were collected in a jeep driven by Jackie Beresford.

Cam Houses is no hilltop hamlet. It has a relatively snug situation, though one of the farmer's wives told me: "We'd had some grim winters. I always say that each winter at Cam Houses, I grow an extra skin!"

At the turn of the century, Greenfield, which gives its name to one of the two becks that form the river Wharfe, was a shooting estate owned by H. Garnett Orme, of Tarn House, Skipton. He and his bride spent a (winter) honeymoon at Greenfield, travelling from Skipton to Horton-in-Ribblesdale. So much snow lay on the fells that walls were overblown and they decided to cross to Greenfield using a a horse-drawn sled. They did not have to open a single gate.

I do not care much for large forests composed of immigrant trees like sitka spruce and lodgepole pine, but after walking on open fells, it was a change to be in Greenfield Forest, where "exotic" species from the New World had the company of such hardy natives as alder and rowan.

Greenfield Forest of 2,000 acres, at an elevation of about 1,500 ft., spreads itself across the wide bowl between the hills. When the ground was first fenced off for tree-planting, and the sheep were kept out, there was a flush of native plants, including drifts of globe flowers. The forest area still has its botanical treasures, for some areas have been left open.

Greenfield Meadow, which is a Site of Special Scientific Interest, has species-rich marsh, meadow and flush habitats, set within a matrix of less rich meadowland that has been semi-improved for agriculture. On the steeper banks and alongside Greenfield Beck grow sneezewort, marsh orchid, bird's eye primrose and meadow saxifrage.

A tract of fen is enlivened by tufted hairgrass, soft rush, lady's mantle, water avens, bogbean and marsh violet. In calcareous flushes grow the Grass of Parnassus and the common butterwort.

Years ago, with Stan Lythe of Grassington, I photographed a nest of short-eared owls. It was Stan's nature to be helpful. He had spent many hours, with permission, watching the owls and trying to locate the nest on tussocky ground. Then he put a small canvas-covered structure at a spot overlooking the nest. This was the hide from which his photography would take place.

I recall using the hide and the mounting excitement I felt as, Stan having left me, I awaited the return of one of the parent birds. It arrived soundlessly and stared about it with large unblinking eyes before ripping up a field vole and delicately feeding it to its young.

Another time, with Stan, I watched an afternoon display by blackcock on a rounded hill near the Greenfield road. The turkey-like birds arrived from different directions at about the same time, a testimony to the accuracy of their diurnal "clocks".

Spring was in the air. The blackcock were here with one object in mind – to mate with the visiting females, who would otherwise have nothing to do with them. The competition was fierce. Blackcock faced up against blackcock and the pairs of suitors put on their most fearsome appearances and aggressive sounds.

The blackcock were here to display, with the object of securing some prime space on the lek [from the Swedish leka, meaning "to play"]. The most successful birds were most likely to be allowed to court the hen birds when they arrived at the lek.

I thought of Stan's flair as a naturalist when I began a new day in tree cover but over-looking the lekking ground, a tract of rough pasture with coarse grasses and rushes. The population of black grouse has been declining fast, but half a dozen cock birds arrived. The two nearest birds faced each other, inflated their red wattles, drooped their dark wings and extended the white undertail coverts.

The blackcock is a big bird, weighing some four pounds, and these two made quite a show as they pranced. They see-sawed, one bird extending its head and neck towards the other bird, which simultaneously drew back. As the first bird retracted its head, so the head and neck of the other was extended.

These two aggressive males hissed and coo-ed, the sounds being like something from primeval times. I watched a blackcock stretch its neck upwards, throw back its head and hiss – *chuwai, chuwai*. This sound has been described as "an explosive sneeze" and to me it suggests air rushing from a cycle tyre on the sudden removal of the valve. Strange bubbling notes – *roo-koo-roo* – were not unlike the cooing of a pigeon.

Across the beck, a roe deer was browsing, oblivious to the hub-hub on the lek.

From Cam Houses, I regained the Pennine Way, which headed for a shoulder of Dodd Fell (2,192 ft). This hill is like a huge sponge, retaining water and releasing it slowly down innumerable gills or sikes, some of which have intriguing names – Old Wife, Nettle Hole and Lady Fold.

5

HAWES
AND HARDRAW

A peaty track leads me along the side of Dodd Fell and down to Gaudy Lane. At Gayle, I examine a "welly gate", and at Hawes I discover the names of men who built a church which casts a shadow over the Pennine Way. I join the market throng and then take the field route to Hardraw.

A south-easterly wind brought me the tang of peat. I knew I was nearing civilisation when the air was flavoured by good muck which was being spread on meadowland near Gayle.

The track along the side of Dodd Fell is so elevated, at 1,870 ft., it might almost be classified as a mountain pass. Military jets were playing hide-and-seek among the fells. A trickle of Pennine Wayfarers brought life to this ancient route, though the only person heading southwards, a middle-aged man, was blundering.

He told me he set off on the Coast to Coast walk, going from east to west, and then decided to switch to the Pennine Way. Now he was toying with the idea of using the Dales Way and heading for the fleshpots of Bowness.

A man who was northward-bound, carrying a pack which included a lightweight tent, had begun the long walk in a snowstorm.Two days later, his companion declared himself whacked – which is not surprising after crossing clarty ground on the Southern Pennines – and he went home. The survivor quickened his pace when I confirmed the presence of a fish and chip shop at Hawes. A young couple who had been snowed off resumed the walk after a few days spent at Hebden Bridge and were now going strongly.

The Pennine Way was, for a short stretch, confined between crumbling limestone walls. Ivor Brown called the moor-and-fell top route "the Great North Roof". I recalled its official opening, at a gathering on Malham Moor, and a chat I had with Tom Stephenson, Secretary of the Ramblers' Association, who had outlined the idea of a Pennine walk in a newspaper article. At the gathering was Tom's great friend, Arthur Raistrick, who was an authority on Dales life and industry.

To use any other name than Pennine Way would be unthinkable though another great fell-walker, Wainwright, thought of it as partly the Pennine Way and partly the Cheviot Way. He was the man who arranged with mine-host at Kirk Yetholm to provide each person who completed the route with a refreshing pint at his [Wainwright's] expense.

I thought of friends who had walked the 250 miles in over a fortnight, glorying in the wide views, and of runners and cyclists who completed the journey in three or four days.

This wild area had not yet received its full springtime complement of birds but the caretakers – the old crows – were up there, one of them honking like an old-type motor horn. The crows nest in isolated thorns and rowans, lagging their nests with sheep wool.

An early lark ascended and sang. The aria was drowned by the engine of a wall-hopping jet aircraft but when the sound waves had receded the bird was still singing. I hoped it had a good nesting season.

At Ten End Peat Ground, a small cairn had been used as a signpost. Some brief directions – to the Cam Road (left) and the Pennine Way (straight on) had been daubed on the loose stones. The Pennine Way itself was now waymarked by cairns.

In Gaudy Lane, near Gayle, I expected to see the dry stones of the walls painted in primary colours. The name, which is derived from Gaudy House, soon gives way to the less exciting title of Moss Lane. I followed a path through meadows, using squeezer-stiles, to emerge among Council houses at Gayle.

The Pennine Way, in its progress through the fields, had been mainly flagged. One of the small gates on a stile was hinged with the soles cut from redundant wellingtons. They worked well, keeping the gate pressed hard against the wall and thus discouraging sheep from passing from one pasture to another.

There must have been Life in the Dales before the introduction of wellies and binder twine – but it cannot have amounted to much. A Dales farmer was a pioneer of re-cycling. He found a ready use for the soles of wellies. One farmer wears a green welly on one foot and a black one on the other. He told me it was not unusual – his son had such a pair!

The welly-gate was devised many years ago and is now ubiquitous. It has a variant in the Dunlop or Michelin gate, made of pieces of old tyre and serving precisely the same purpose – that of ensuring that the stile gate closes behind a walker with a decisive "clunk".

I had a snack meal overlooking the ford above the waterfalls at Gayle. The water looked deep and was flowing swiftly, but local farmers forded the beck in their vehicles without a moment's hesitation, startling the ducks.

When I saw cars arriving from the breezy heights of Fleet Moss (at 1,934 ft the highest road in North Yorkshire) I felt a glow of achievement at having walked. From Gayle, I bestrode a flagged path through a field running down to Duerley Beck, which had gone white with fury after recent rain. The beck was descending a natural staircase formed of beds of limestone.

Soon the tower and "pepper pot" turret of Hawes Church were in view. The turret is not just an embellishment; it has the practical use of containing the steps leading to the top of the tower.

In a leaflet dealing with the history of the Church was an eye-witness account by Edward Moore of the building of the Church. It was a late-comer, the foundation stone being laid in the summer of 1850. There was an easy informality about the prose: "The resident architect was named Dixon, and he lodged with Betty Scarr all the time it was being built. The builders' names were Edmund Dick, Dick Fothergill, John Jeff and Lang Anty; they had two labourers or hod carriers, Jimmy Kelly and Little Peter, both Irishmen...

"Ralph Stockdale carted all the freestone from the top of Snaizefell; it was brought from the top down the road in Lang Gill on a sort of sledge. When the last stone was fixed on the top of the turret, Peter stood on it on one foot, waving the other and also his arms to amuse the spectators below..."

It being market day (Tuesday), Hawes was a-wash with gossip. A local was saying: "I've told my 'lot' that I don't want to be a financial burden to 'em when I'm old; I'd much rayther be a financial burden while I'm young enough to enjoy it." A parson with high-church ideas was reported to be having his congregation "bobbing up and down like a lot of tappets".

Grave-looking farmers – of the type that J. B. Priestley likened to "minor characters from Ibsen" – thronged the auction mart. The auctioneer introduced some stock with the time-honoured words: "Now then, gentlemen, here we have..." Bidding began. The voice of the auctioneer quickened to a machine-gun chatter, which I found it hard to follow. The farmers and dealers understood him perfectly.

Most transactions are accompanied by an extra, private monetary arrangement summed

Hawes church and a section of the Pennine Way.

Farmstead near Gayle.

up in the Dales as "a bit o' luck". It has been so since pre-mart days, when dealings took place in the main street and farmers arrived with pockets full of sovereigns. A farm man who deputised for his master, who was ill, returned with a new tup. His master did not seem pleased with his choice of animal. "It's getten a pedigree," said the farm man. And the farmer, sighing deeply, said: "By gow, it needs one!"

At Hawes, the auctioneer on the rostrum could not afford to relax for a second. His eyes moved restlessly, seeking to detect the subtle signs of interest in the human throng. One old chap was bidding with a movement of one finger, which he slyly concealed from the man who stood next to him. Another rubbed a finger up and down his nose. Hardly anyone put a bid into words.

At the refreshment room, where I had tea and buttered scones, I was reminded of the farm man who, visiting Hawes, went to a cafe in the market hall and, when no instruction was given, was asked if he would like beans on toast. "Aw reight", he said, "if thou hasn't getten any plates." Another man, shown the menu, is said to have uttered but one word — "yes".

Wensleydale, unlike most valleys, is open-ended. I know that other dales have roads leading out at each end, but Wensleydale's roads do not go mountaineering; it is like driving through a broad trough between ice-sculpted fells. The main road from Leyburn goes straight through to Sedbergh, with a branch at the "Moorcock" leading to Mallerstang and Kirkby Stephen.

At Hawes, isolation has bred independence and also a deep local pride. This town is not conurbated and stands about 16 miles from each of a ring of towns — Sedbergh, Kirkby Stephen, Ingleton and Leyburn. When I wrote my first article in "The Dalesman" about Hawes, in 1955, I concentrated on its Market, which I described as being at the tail-end of a long tradition. The wind whistled down a street that did not contain more than a dozen stalls and (I was told) often had but half that number.

In 1955, farmers' wives were persuading their husbands to take them by car to Darlington and other large shopping centres. They certainly could not go by train, for the Wensleydale line had already been closed to passenger traffic.

The growth of Hawes was stimulated by the award of a market charter in 1699 (not 1700, as mentioned in some books). This town had humble beginnings. Early in the 14th century, there may have been little more than a tiny settlement in the wide-flung Forest of Wensleydale. Hawes was then part of the parish of Aysgarth. In the 15th century, the modest settlement acquired a chapel of ease. Hawes received its parish status in the 17th century.

The place grew in size and importance as a halt on a busy packhorse route. Then came the Richmond-Lancaster turnpike, diverted from its high route, to be followed in 1878 by the aforementioned Wensleydale Railway. From the station at Hawes was despatched milk in kits and milk processed into the famous Wensleydale cheese. Another export was Burtersett flagstones, consigned to the burgeoning towns of East Lancashire.

Yet Hawes retained its village atmosphere. I used to visit the obscurely-situated offices of the Aysgarth Rural District Council, approached by a flight of wooden steps. The staff numbered three and the product of a penny rate was — £34.

Hawes Market Hall was run on puritanical lines. There must be no hanky-panky, and certainly no gambling. When bingo became a craze, someone tried to hire the Hall for this purpose, only to be politely but firmly told that it would not be allowed. A notice at the Penny Garth — now used for car parking — prohibited the playing of games here on a Sunday.

Hawes main street (D.G. Mather).

Duerley Beck, Gayle (W.A. Hayward).

Kit Calvert, the "compleat dalesman", whose memory for t'auld days was encyclopaedic, saved the local cheese factory in the 1930s when it was threatened with closure. Kit's bookshop, run as a glorified hobby, met a local need. It was referred to by Mr. Mason, an elderly voluntary helper, as "Hawes University".

The bookshop had the musty flavour imparted by old and damp books. Most of them were soppy romances or Victorian stories with a strong religious flavour. If there was no one in attendance, a purchaser left the money in a chapel collection tray. Or a note was left on a round table which held a Bible, open at Proverbs. The note instructed the buyer of a book to "contact Mr. C. Chapman, grocer, next door". Mr. Chapman put the money in an old tin box and it awaited collection by Kit.

Kit was always about on Market Day. His cronies turned up at the bookshop from near and far. The reek of black twist burning in a clay pipe seared the throats of strangers as they pushed their way between the locals with the object of buying books.

I left Hawes sucking an ice cream. I used the footpath way, through the fields to the river bridge. I looked at the wayward river Ure and recalled a great angling writer, Tim Wilson, who used to tell me about the Wensleydale men who went looking for crayfish, "those freshwater lobsters".

As far as Tim could discover, it was only in the Ure that crayfish were protected by having a close season. Both the Wensleydale and the Hawes and High Abbotside Angling Association had a by-law stipulating that "the cray fishing season shall begin on August 10th and end on September 30th." They also charged a shilling for a cray-fishing ticket. What was good sport to one person was "a fiddling job" to another. Only the claws and flippers held edible flesh and after the crayfish had been boiled the claws were cracked with a hammer. Ugh!

Tim told me of going cray-fishing with a Hawes friend on the low side of Sandy Wheel. Liver was used as bait; it was cut into six pieces and tied to a yard of string and a stick. The lures were positioned on the stone-strewn bed of the river and soon the crayfish were appearing. Fourteen of them collected round a single bait and all but two were safely netted.

Sproates Blades, the best-known of the old anglers of the Hawes district, was commissioned to provide 1,000 live crayfish for the stocking of a Scottish reservoir. He was paid £10 for the job. The required number were obtained in under two hours' work one evening and the crayfish were kept alive in bags sunk in Gayle Beck. Next day, they were transported north in milk kits and all arrived safely.

At Hardraw, I paid a small sum at the *Green Dragon Hotel* for admission to Hardraw Force. I have often wondered about the dragon which is portrayed with imaginative zest on the hotel signboard. Was it connected with heraldry or some folk tale? Had the story of the green dragon begun with the discovery of a fossil, which was the story told to me by a member of the local Rotary Club when I gave a talk some years ago?

I thought nothing more of it until, reading a piece about Hardraw by David Leather, I made the acquaintance of *Magapezia*, an armoured flesh-eating amphibian whose fossilised footprints, found by a Bradford school party in rock associated with the Lower Carboniferous period, are estimated to be 335 million years old. These are, it is thought, the oldest tracks of a four-legged animal yet found in Britain.

The path I followed to Hardraw Force had a woodland setting. I passed between shrubs and trees holding out buds or catkins. A dipper flew off with its metallic cries – *zit, zit, zit*. Jackdaws rendered a chorus of metallic calls, as though anxious that they should be heard above the boom of the water.

Hardraw Scar (Karl Stedman).

Not until I was close to the tumbling water, and its sound was impressively large, did I see the spectacle of a beck leaping from the lip of a 100 ft cliff. The water did not encounter an obstruction all the way down to its plunge pool. I have seen a photograph taken in 1881 of Hardraw frozen from top to bottom as an enormous pillar of ice.

Clearly delineated on the cliff which provided an impressive background to the fall was a complete cycle of the Yoredale Series of rocks – from top to bottom, Hardraw limestone, sand-stone and shales. I saw a young couple standing apparently in the midst of the waterfall, whereas they were on a wide ledge immediately behind.

Hardraw is famous for its tumbling water. It was during the Romantic Age (1780-1840) that such a natural spectacle was visited, drawn, painted and commended by intrepid travellers who published details of their journeys. They prompted others to tour the Dales, visiting the recommended sights.

William and Dorothy Wordsworth were here in the winter of 1799; they walked round the back of the waterfall and wrote of the icicles seen hanging from the rocks above that they were "lofty and magnificent". Turner, the painter, sketched with the object of painting the waterfall when he had reflected on it. Hardraw Force became so famous that an engraving of it appeared on the notes of the local bank.

The coming of the railway to Hawes last century brought tourists en masse, especially as band contests were held in the natural amphitheatre of the ravine down which the Hardraw beck made its way. Dr. J. Sutcliffe Smith, in his "Music of the Yorkshire Dales" (1930), called Hardraw "the battlefield of bands" and described the setting as "an ideal, ready-made open-air concert room, with an auditorium capable of holding 30,000 people, the like of which is probably not to be found elsewhere in Great Britain".

In June 1903, special trains brought brass band enthusiasts from as far away as Manchester and Scarborough. The bands, on arriving at Hawes by train, usually played while walking down the main street and then clambered on to wagonettes to be conveyed across the dale to Hardraw. Tents were erected for the sale of refreshments and "into t'teens o' Bobbies" were drafted in to maintain law and order, though it was an orderly throng. "People came to listen to t'bands."

The band contests have been revived in recent years. Now, instead of arriving by train, the bands and their supporters turn up in buses and cars which create much more of a parking problem.

I enjoy a good band but prefer to go to Hardraw on a quiet day in spring or autumn. Charles Fothergill (1805) benefited from having the company of a local man, Thomas Harrison, who entertained him with tales, though he did have rather a lot of accounts of "those unfortunates who had perished by falling over the scar or precipice". Fothergill observed that "here as at other high falls of water, there are beautiful rainbow-like reflections created by the sun beams operating on the spray that rises to a great height".

Forty years ago, John William Sharples of Hardraw told me of a cloudburst over Great Shunner Fell and its effect on Hardraw Force. He said: "I was only a young man at the time and was working at a quarry in Garsdale, but I'd lamed myself and was off work. I was living at Scar End at the time, so I'd a wonderful chance of seeing the storm.

"I've never seen so much water come down as that particular day, and the *Green Dragon* pub was flooded out. There was water nearly half way up t'walls in the lower rooms and half a foot o' mud on t'floors. I saw a horse standing belly deep in a stable opposite, and some pigs next door swam out o' t'building over bottom half o' t'door. They escaped down yon fields.

Signpost at Hawes.

Seventeenth century doorhead in Hawes.

"It was July. The storm came after dinner. Aye – there was thunderin' and lightnin' every minute and hail stones as big as marbles. Fish were swept from t'river on to t'banks, and on t'low side of Hardraw, meadows were covered with mud. Hardraw Bridge was swept away and iron railings were bent by t'rush o' watter".

The cafe where I refreshed myself had souvenirs of the dales, including the framed photographs of sheep. I ate under the unblinking gaze of lordly Swaledales, or Sward'ls, to use the local pronunciation. Then it was off to the "attic" of Wensleydale – the summit cairn of Great Shunner Fell.

Old farmstead, upper Swaledale.

A pattern of drystone walls near Gunnerside.

6

SKYLINE ROUTE
TO SWALEDALE

The Pennine Way leads me over Great Shunner Fell, where I meet a particularly "tame" grouse and see an army of "stone men". At Thwaite I seek out the birthplace of the Kearton brothers – pioneers of wildlife photography – and cross the "island hill" of Kisdon on my way to Keld.

The ascent of Great Shunner Fell began in sunshine. Then a storm, which was being brewed up much further north, bore down on me, reminding me of Mr. Sharples' tale of the day when Hardraw was almost washed away.

A blue-black cloud spread until it occupied half the sky. The breeze slackened, an ominous sign. Then Great Shunner warded off the cloud and it tracked down Swaledale, as though intent on watering the gardens of Reeth and Richmond.

Dalesfolk of old, having outdoor occupations, regulated their lives by the weather and had their own terms for aspects of it – snizy, for raw; clashy, which is turbulent and very wet; and glisky for a day that starts off excessively bright: a brightness which doesn't last.

The signpost at Hardraw indicated THWAITE (PENNINE WAY) 8. The rising gradient offered no respite to my stiffened limbs. At Bluebell Hill, 1,000 ft above sea level, the track – after dallying between walls – burst on to the open fell. Dorothy and William Wordsworth were familiar with the heights of Great Shunner. She wrote in her Journal for October, 1802: "Before we got upon the bare hills, there was a hunting lodge on our right...with fir plantations about."

The fell route was not hard to pick out, such was the pounding it had received from Pennine Wayfarers. Cairns were commonplace. The writer J.H.B. Peel saw so many cairns, he found it wearisome to count them. The walking was pleasant, "the going is good, over firm turf, with the world falling away from either side, pastoral on the left, moorish on the right."

Ingleborough, represented by a dove-grey form, with the familiar flat top, was in the sunny half of the sky.

I saw shelves of limestone, holding the promise, in weeks to come, of an array of attractive flowers. I was aware of the grinding and polishing properties of a glacier that trundles across a landscape. No hard edges are apparent. Wensleydale was left with a comfortable U-shape between smooth-sided fells.

A rambler, who was having an early snack, referred to it as "butty stop". He lifted a sandwich from a yellow plastic container with a picture of Santa Claus on the lid, and lamented that his children had "pinched" the more respectable food boxes of his household.

Great Shunner was not a hard climb. Peel wrote of the track that "at Crag End Beacon it becomes mountainous, and at Great Shunner Fell it pauses for breath." The fell bore the classic marks of over-use by ramblers. Boots had broken through the thin skin of the earth. Travellers were taking wider and wider courses to avoid the peat-dubs.

Near a tarnlet – it was not much more than a large but permanent puddle – I had an interlude stalking a "tame" grouse. This bird, a cock bird, was reticent to fly. The rich browns of its plumage contrasted with the almost white grasses which, through excessive sheep grazing, have taken over from the heather on many a Pennine fell.

The red grouse is a Dales stay-at-home, and would therefore be a worthy emblem for the area. It is dependent on heather for cover and for food. Only when there is that cruel combination of snow crusted with ice is it forced to leave its native moors. Then the dales-folk see displaced and dispirited grouse perched on walls near the farms and villages.

How does the grouse manage to digest the tough heather fare? Its beak is not very large but must have pincer-like strength. In winter, the thick plumage is augmented by white feathering on the legs – by avian spats, indeed!

In its bleak upland haunt, the grouse's nesting success is closely related to the weather. Cold and wet conditions are bad for new-hatched chicks. They depend largely on the abundance of moorland insects, so moist conditions are important. Autumn brings to the grouse family a bounty of berries, to fatten them up before the ritual slaughter which begins on the Glorious Twelfth.

"My" Shunner Fell grouse wearied of being peered at from close range. When I was beginning to think it must be injured and incapable of flight, the bird seemed to explode into life and went off with a flurry of wings. The crowing call – *kowa, kowa, kowa* – roused all the moorland echoes.

Stevenson wrote of a "vacant, wine-red moor". Great Shunner Fell is not exclusively under heather and it is certainly not vacant, holding sheep and the upland waders, such as golden plover, dunlin and curlew. It was not "vacant" in t'auld days, judging by the way a mineralised area was exploited by t'auld man, a collective name for past generations of lead-miners.

Visitors with a surfeit of energy have created a "stone army" on the stretch of fell towards Buttertubs Pass. Here there is a large patch of handy slabs of gritstone which are almost as good as Lego in the hands of a careful builder. The "stone men" are cairns, of course. From a distance, the many neat heaps of gritstone give the impression of being an altar to some ancient earth-god.

At 2,350 ft., having reached the summit of the sprawling mass of gritstone, peat and heather, I celebrated with thermos tea and waited for the last of the storm cloud to be wafted slowly eastwards along the valley of the Swale. It left the atmosphere so clean and crisp that far to the north I saw the huge bulk of Cross Fell.

A walker, ending his climb of Great Shunner with a storming finish, staggered up the loose stones of the cairn and raised his arm, simultaneously shouting "bingo!"

The map showed the Pennine Way as descending between Burnt Hill and Little Shunner Fell. The area had names evoking its dark and soggy nature – Black Hill and Black Bank, Whetstone Rigg and Blaeberry Head, Coal Syke and Benty Gutter, also a feature named – Boots! The "whetstone" was, of course, used for sharpening scythes.

The moorland was pitted with shake-holes or swallow-holes, which are green funnels created over limestone by a seepage of material through fissures in the rock. A meadow pipit hopped around as though trying to infuse a little life on to a hillside where the vegetation was sere.

Thwaite Common drains into Thwaite Beck which hastens to meet the Swale. Reedy, peaty uplands give way to a neat pattern of drystone walls, enfolding the meadows of Thwaite Side. Now, in spring, they were overspread with "muck" from the cattle which over-winter in the byres. Later, they would be spangled with flowers. The "flower fields" of Thwaite are famous.

I walked down into an area where placenames are predominantly Old Norse. Thwaite is from "thveit", which means a clearing. Muker, the next village down the dale, is derived from "mjor-akr", or small field. Gunnerside comes from "saetr" (the shieling or place of

Two views of sheep judging at Muker Show.

Upper Swaledale farmer.

summer pasture, this one belonging to Mr. Gunnar). The topographical names have a generous sprinkling of Old Norse – fell, from fjall, and force, from fors, meaning a waterfall, as I had observed at Hardraw.

I strode through Thwaite to where the stonework about the door of a cottage was seen to be carved with the figures of birds and beasts. Here, too, were initials RK and CK, representing Richard Kearton and his brother, Cherry. These two dalesmen, the sons of a Swaledale gamekeeper, have an honourable place in the realm of natural history as pioneers of bird photography.

Richard Kearton was proud of his ancestry and achievements. His autobiography, published in 1926 as "A Naturalist's Pilgrimage", was proclaimed to be "a romance of real life, or how a Shepherd Boy became England's Premier Lecturer".

Richard, born on January 2, 1862, came from yeoman stock. The Keartons had owned land in Swaledale since the 14th century. Richard was one of the four sons of John and Mary Kearton (who also had two daughters, Jane and Margaret). When he was a young man, the lead mines were operating. Farming, as yet unmechanised, "toughened the steel in my character".

Richard fell out of a tree while bird-nesting but this stocky, crippled lad who grew up with limited horizons achieved international eminence.

As a young man in Swaledale, he "salved" sheep with a mixture of Norway tar and Irish butter. He said that his basic accomplishment was helping to "make a couple of nourishing blades of grass grow where only one struggled for existence before".

How the son of a poor country gamekeeper came to write pioneering works on natural history is a story that began on Muker Moor, in the early autumn of 1882. George Brook, who rented the Moor, invited Sidney Galpin, one of the founders of Cassell, then the largest publishing house in the world, to join him for the grouse-shooting.

The party arrived at Bull Bog, near the Buttertubs, and Richard, who was helping, offered to call up an old cock grouse for Galpin. "We retired to a deep gully in the peat moss, and in a few moments I brought along an old moorcock, which was promptly bagged by as pretty a cross shot as I ever saw fired in all my life".

Galpin, impressed by Richard's bright manner, offered him a job in a business department of Cassell's, his first task being to address envelopes and wrappers, for 14s a week. Six years later, he was the assistant manager.

He had renewed his interest in bird life. Invited to write about nests and eggs for "Swaysland's Familiar Wild Birds", which would be illuminated by Archibald Thorburn and others, he obliged, but the book was never published. Richard was allowed to complete his own part of the work, and to see it through the press as "Eggs and Egg-collecting". He was paid three guineas – for a book that was to go through 19 editions.

Cherry Kearton joined his brother at Cassell's and their interest in the countryside was further stimulated when Cherry bought a second-hand camera. On April 10, 1892, while staying with some Yorkshire friends near Enfield, Richard found a song thrush nest and invited Cherry to photograph it.

The result was so full of promise that Richard wrote a book on birds' nests, illustrating it with photographs taken "direct from nature", which was made possible by adopting the new American half-tone method of reproducing pictures.

Three words – "direct from nature" – were to be the theme of their later work. In short, and by chance, Richard and Cherry Kearton produced what I believe to be the first natural history books illustrated by photographs.

The brothers must have groaned under the weight of their photographic equipment. The first attempts made by Richard to obtain pictures of birds at the nest without disturbing them were bizarre, involving "hides", such as a hollow ox and sheep. One "hide" represented part of a tree trunk. They even made a hollow representation of a rock.

To obtain pictures of merlins nesting on the moor in his native Swaledale, Richard put the camera in a representation of a (recumbent) sheep. He ran a wire to a hidey-hole in a shelter made of turves of peat. All went well, until the farmer turned up with his dog, which rounded up all the sheep except one – Richard's.

It was discovered that the actual shape of the "hide" did not matter. Any hollow structure was suitable. It must be erected and moved up to the nest in stages over several days. Two people must go to the hide and one return. The Keartons had become aware of an important fact – that most birds cannot count.

After collaborating with Richard in several important books relating to the wilder regions of Britain and Ireland, Cherry went off to Africa. Richard's autobiography was reviewed by "Punch" in verse:

> Here a real romance is told
> (Fact in this form fiction betters)
> How a herd-boy left the fold,
> How he won a place in letters;
> Loving much, beloved of Pan –
> Bird and beast and fellow man.

I have a batch of letters written by Richard Kearton, in his last days, to a young Lancashire ornithologist. They are most entertaining, especially when Richard urged his correspondent not to take up cine-photography but to remain true to his old plate camera. He could not see a future for "moving pictures"!

From Thwaite, it was an easy stroll to Muker, where memorials to the Kearton brothers adorn the outside wall of the former school. Muker is the setting for my favourite Dales show. Here, in early autumn, while the famous brass band plays, sheepdogs are put through their paces.

A competitor in the sheepdog trial uses cool, clear whistles to direct a collie and sprightly hill sheep through a trials routine which consists of negotiating three pairs of hurdles and directing the sheep into a pen.

The last time I watched, I was aware of the considerable tension for dog, sheep and handler as the pen was approached. When the sheep were inside, and the gate had been closed, one sheep was still frisky enough to leap straight out without touching the top bar.

The Dales reek of sheep. At Muker Show was an assembly of outstanding animals. Every tup, with its dark face, grey muzzle and curving horns, resembled the majestic "Rastus the Ram" emblem of the Dales National Park.

Attending Muker Show is, for me, a regular prelude to a visit to Kisdon, a favourite hill, which lies between Muker and Keld. I had been uncertain whether to use the footpath through the meadows, from Thwaite to Keld, or to cross the hill. In the end it was the "high road" I favoured.

The "island hill" of Kisdon, by retaining its heather, has a small community of red grouse. The Celts named the hill and an 18th century cartographer referred to it as "Kisdon Island".

The Kisdon grouse were in "breeding mode". Spring is the time to watch our hardy "moorcock". I had a ringside view of a tussle between two well-matched grouse. The home

River Swale and Kisdon.

Barns, ancient and modern, near Muker.

The old institute at Muker.

bird pursued the incoming bird. When it did not yield, the contest began. Wings and claws were used as weapons. Feathers flew!

At the closing stage of my Kisdon walk, I viewed the gorge down which the Swale flows. To anyone using the dale road from Muker to Keld, or indeed the field path between those two villages, this area "back o' Kisdon" will be as mysterious as the dark side of the moon. Camden, centuries ago, commented that the Swale "rusheth rather than runneth". In the gorge, it also tumbleth!

Kisdon is crossed by the Corpse Way, a track used by relatives and friends bearing the bodies of those who had died at the dalehead and must be buried at Grinton, which then was the only consecrated ground in the dale. T. D. Whitaker, the historian, wrote of how "the bodies were conveyed for burial upon men's shoulders upwards of twelve miles to the parish church, not in coffins but in rude wicker baskets."

In due course, a church and graveyard were available at Muker. One burial here that was difficult to organise concerned the mother of the aforementioned Richard and Cherry Kearton, for she died at the home of a daughter at Nateby, near Kirkby Stephen.

Richard had promised her that she would be interred at Muker, but on the appointed day a blizzard raged, drifting on the wild upland road between Mallerstang and Swaledale. A horse and sled were hired, the sled being the hearse. The funeral party was headed by men with spades who cut through the drifts. Muker was reached, the interment took place and the chilled mourners returned safely to Nateby.

Kisdon is a Hill for All Seasons. One winter, in crisp snow, I walked along the high path east of the Swale at what dalesfolk call the "edge o' dark". The Hill was little more than a silhouette. A pheasant spread snow with vigorous leg movements and dined on – who knows what?

A black grouse was guzzling some wizened thorn berries. Big Big Alderson, of Angram, used to tell me of the huge flocks of black grouse seen descending on the berried trees of the fellsides during a cold snap.

At first light in spring, the blue-black birds, which resemble "little turkeys", display to each other, cooing and hissing. I had been at a lek during my visit to Greenfield Forest, near Cam Houses. The bird that coos and hisses the most gets the best ground – and also the female of the species.

One of the joys of taking the field path to Keld is to be aware of the fellside economy and our inheritance of stone structures – farmsteads, drystone walls and diminutive field barns, all built of native materials. They blend with the landscape, unlike the modern buildings made of breeze- blocks and corrugated zinc, which resemble aircraft hangers.

Nowhere in the Dales are field barns to be seen in greater numbers and such diversity as in upper Swaledale. Sixty-three such buildings stand within a half-mile radius of Muker. Cash is available in the form of grants to protect the old barn-and-wall landscape of the National Park. The restoration scheme began in April, 1989. Both Swaledale and Arkengarthdale have been designated as a conservation area.

Bill Alderson used to tell me that when he was a lad such field barns were used for tying-up young stock in winter. His father would ask him to call at several barns on his way to school at Muker. Bill's job was to give the cattle hay and his father followed in his footsteps and let the stock out to drink at the spring. Father also "mucked out" the cowhouse.

In Swaledale, a barn cum tying up place for stock is spoken of as a "field house", but "cowhouse" is a commoner and more exact term, which is supplanted by "laithe" in parts of Wensleydale and upper Wharfedale.

The field barn of the upper dales belonged to the age of small-time agriculture, being associated with one or two small fields – a scale of operation which could be managed by one man with the help of a horse and various types of sled.

Into the barn went hay made on the adjacent land. From the barn was taken "muck", the droppings of the cattle which had become mixed with the bracken or straw that provided bedding. "Muck" was sledded to where it could be dumped across the land as small heaps and then spread finely by hand-fork.

Though small, the barn thus met a specific requirement in the Norse-type stock-rearing routine of the hill country. No two barns are exactly alike. A basic plan is apparent, but proportions vary and so does the quality of the workmanship.

Some barns have mortared walls and others were built of "dry" stones. Some were given "proper" foundations and others merely rested on the ground. A number of barns have lean-to buildings to enable more stock to be kept. Such additions do not add to their visual appeal, for they were invariably roofed with corrugated iron, which has now rusted.

In the heyday of the field barns, cattle were tied up from November until May. They were released briefly during the day to go to water. Arthur Young, the writer about agriculture, who visited Swaledale in the later part of the 18th century, noted that in winter the cows were fed on hay alone, "of which they eat one and a-half acre per head". This explains why the area in which the cattle were housed is quite small in relation to the size of the building.

The field path from Thwaite to Keld runs by Dirty Piece and Skeb Skeugh, approaching – but not quite reaching – the scattering of houses at Angram and then switching direction to climb a hillside towards a disused quarry and the Kisdon track. Keld's telephone kiosk has a prominent position and is seen from vantage points miles away.

Keld means "spring". The village has "one road in and one road out". Everywhere is the sound of tumbling water at Catrake and Kisdon Forces. Wainwath Falls, the most picturesque, are best-seen from a bridge which takes the road to West Stonesdale and Tan Hill across the Swale.

In the 1850s, Walter White saw few wayfarers. "Perhaps a boy trudges by, pulling a donkey, which drags a sledge laden with turf or hay; or a pedlar with crockery; but for miles your only living companions are sheep and geese."

Characteristic barns and drystone walls in Swaledale.

Thwaite village and Kisdon.

Tan Hill Show, above Swaledale.

7

LEAD MINE
COUNTRY

I pass Crackpot Hall and ponder on the mining and miners of upper Swaledale. A wren welcomes me to a gorge where I find a "kirk" situated behind a waterfall. Following a moorland trod, I reach Gunnerside Gill, which is tenanted by the ghosts of long-dead miners. At Old Gang, I see the remnants of smelt mill and peat store and watch a woodcock carrying one of its young.

Kraa! Kraa! Kraa! The voice of a crow, heard back o' Kisdon, had a peevish edge to it. I had dined near East Gill Force, where the seething water ran as white as milk. I plodded along a path high above the Swale. A red dot, far below, proved to be the anorak of a visitor who was standing near Kisdon Force.

The crow's husky voice was a timely reminder, as I made for the ruins of Crackpot Hall and Swinnergill, that crackpot is derived from the Old Norse "kraka", and the name thus means a pothole frequented by crows, or possibly ravens. (This Crackpot should not be confused with that opposite Gunnerside).

At Crackpot, I was in Lead Mine Country. "They" do say that Swaledale lead covered the roof of St. Peter's in Rome. It was mined in Roman times and a once great industry petered out locally towards the end of last century, since when a few men have riddled through the spoil heaps for barytes.

When the ruins of Crackpot Hall came into sight, I was reminded of a visit with Matthew Cherry, of Gunnerside, when we found a blacksmith's forge intact and complete with bellows.

The old building stands in "tewit country", and a lapwing wailed from a pasture as I strolled by. Where old walls and grey screes are plentiful, the stean-chat [wheatear] dips and calls.

Crackpot Hall was built by Lord Wharton and held by him and his family for some 200 years. The property and its outpastures were purchased in 1738 by Thomas Smith, though the Wharton Trustees did not part with the mineral rights on the common land. This led to a legal battle over the right to dig for lead.

In this Lead Mine Country, I had a feeling that every square foot of ground had been crushed by the human foot during the centuries when farming went side by side with mining. The area has innumerable sheep trods, some of which develop into paths. As a dales farmer told me: "Sheep maks 'em. Folks follow 'em. Then they go jiggerly all ower t'place".

I was to see much evidence of t'auld man, the spirit of mining past, during my traverse of this weary landscape. The evidence would come in seeing levels driven into shale or living rock which now had entrances fringed with ferns. I would feel the cold dampness of the mine on my face and see bits of rails and sleepers that were part of a subterranean tramway.

The first sensation, at the mouth of a level, was to hear the dripping of water from arched roofs holding clusters of tiny stalactites, formed of re-deposited limestone. In the gills of upper Swaledale are ruined store places, offices, blacksmith's shops and the lodgings used by miners during the working week.

In a landscape scored by workings are the saucer-like depressions of bell-pits, signifying where lead was found close to the surface. The lead and associated minerals were located mainly in the upper limestone and chert beds of the Yoredale strata. To find galena, or lead ore, in veins or rakes, the miners drove levels and occasionally sank shafts.

Through sheer hard work, in grim conditions, dalesmen honeycombed the hills. So extensive were some of the lead mines that they joined up with each other. It was once possible, with knowledge and confidence, to go underground in Gunnerside Gill and, by following a succession of passages, to emerge in Arkengarthdale, some six miles away.

In winter, the miners saw daylight at week-ends, for during a working day it was dark when they went underground and dark when they returned to the surface. The conditions were grim, with dampness, foul air and a hard type of dust to clog and lacerate their lungs, leading to painful early death from a form of silicosis known as "gruver's complaint".

It was Matthew Cherry, a Swaledale man who returned to his native dale in retirement, who made sense out of the disorder of the post-mining age, with its echoing adits, crumbling buildings, spoil heaps and patches of a starry white flower known as the spring sandwort, which is lead tolerant and grows where land has been disturbed by mining.

The heyday of the industry in the upper Dales was between 1790 and 1860. Many of the mines were closed by 1880. I heard from the Swaledale folk of the "hush", a crude opencast method of finding the veins. The sides of the gills are scored by "hushes", caused when water which had been dammed at the top of the hill was suddenly released to gouge out the upper surface and (hopefully) expose some workable veins.

This was no random operation, being planned with precision. The dam was used repeatedly until all recoverable ore had been taken away. Into the dam was diverted surface water from adjacent areas of moorland. A hush-gutter [v-shaped notch] was cut in the slope between the dam and where the lead vein was believed to lie.

Water in the dam was released from time to time with devastating effect. It scoured the ground, sweeping away loose material and exposing the vein. The miners now set about the mineralised area with crowbars and picks. When they had done what was easily possible, and had loosened some more of the hillside, they returned to the re-filled dam and released more water.

It was a messy business. Much of the material, swept into the beck, found its way down to the river. I shudder to think what effect it would have on the fish and other aquatic life.

The Old Field Hush, a huge scar in the Crackpot area, yielded enormous returns for a group of men who reached an agreement with the mining company in about 1846. The idea was to re-work the hush. The men "struck it rich" and were taking away substantial amounts of lead ore for about 16 years.

In Swaledale, the hills are hollow. A rough map of part of the Fryerfold Vein shows the complexity of the workings which were necessary to follow the fickle veins of workable ore. Names include Puke Sump, Alderson Tripey Waggon Drift, Slack Water Drift and Thompson Water.

A piece of Dales lead weighs heavily in the hand. Frank Beresford, a raconteur with a fund of Dales stories, once showed me such a piece. He allowed me to assess its weight and to examine it closely. Then he told me that this was "Ingleborough" lead, given to him by a friend in Swaledale. The ore had been transported from Ingleborough to Swaledale for smelting.

A smelt mill received the lead after it had been crushed sieved and separated from other minerals by machines operating by waterpower. Large waterwheels were a conspicuous

Langthwaite, Arkengarthdale.

Gunpowder House, near Langthwaite.

feature of the gills and moor edges of Swaledale. At the smelt mill, the ore was heated and its sulphur and other impurities burned off as gases.

Long flues carried the noxious fumes to chimneys on the skyline. They also ensured that deposits of lead which would otherwise be wasted formed on the arches and could be scraped off. The residual metal, poured into moulds, hardened and was turned out as ingots known as "pigs".

Superstition was rife among lead-miners. Edward R Fawcett recorded that an unforgivable sin was to whistle underground, for the shrill sound was supposed to cause the ore to vanish. For some reason, it was unlucky if a tailor visited the mines.

Walter White, a Victorian visitor, overtook a party of miners, boys and men who were going home from work. The boys could read, but only one of them really enjoyed this mental exercise. His father said he was a "good quiet boy" who "likes to sit down wi' his book o' evenin's; t'others say he is tired. He can draw a bit, too; and I'd like well to send 'n to a good skule, but I gets two pounds a month, and that's poor addlings".

A young lad wished that he wasn't so tired after digging lead. Reading made him fall asleep, yet he enjoyed reading. "It don't seem right," he added, "that a lad should want a bit o' larnin' and not get it".

Early in the 18th century, the average Swaledale miner was paid a shilling a day for an eight hour shift. By the first part of the 19th century, the rate had risen to 10s or 12s a day. It was a spartan life, living in a small thatched house, renting some land on which to keep a few domestic animals, including a cow, pig and some hens – and going to work on a breakfast of oatmeal porridge and blue [skimmed] milk.

Nicknames were common to distinguish members of large families. Take the Aldersons as an example. In 1804, there were no less than eight Thomas Aldersons in upper Swaledale, known respectively as Grain Tom, Glowermore Tom, Screamer Tom, Poddish Tom, Tarry Tom, Tish Tom, Tripy Tom and Trooper Tom.

Disturb the old mining records, and details emerge of ancient disputes, such as one affecting the Out Pasture at Crackpot Hall.

In 1767, Parkes and Company (who had the Beldi Hill Mine) sub-let a mining concession in Hall Out Pasture to one Richard Metcalfe, of Calvert Houses, and John Scott, his partner. You will recall that the Wharton Trustees kept the mining rights.

The Wharton Estate had been acquired (through marriage) by Lord Pomfret. His Lordship contended that he, and none other, could grant leases on Hall Out Pasture. Enter Thomas Smith, of Crackpot Hall, who asserted that for many years that land had been a recognised part of his farm.

It was the start of a difference that led to a situation where Lord Pomfret told his men to sink shafts on the ground that had been sub-let to Richard Metcalfe. From these shafts, cross-cuts were made so that the lead vein could be worked. They broke into part of a system which was being worked by their opponents. A fight broke out underground!

When the case came to law, Thomas Smith, of Crackpot Hall, was awarded £400 as compensation for damage caused to his property. The hapless Lord Pomfret, who was already overburdened with debt, was provided with lodgings at the Tower of London.

Beyond Crackpot, I entered Swinnergill, being greeted to this V-shaped valley by the crowing of a cock pheasant. When pheasants were first seen in the upper dale, they were referred to as "them long-tailed birds". So attractive was a pheasant to local families who were accustomed to seeing streaky-brown moorland birds that some pheasants were slain to be "stuffed" and exhibited in glass-fronted cases.

On the Corpse Way near Gunnerside (Tom Sykes).

Gunnerside Gill near Burton Level (J.C. Longstaff).

Lead mining remains in Gunnerside Gill (J.C. Longstaff).

Swinnergill bore all the marks of a busy lead mine. Lord Pomfret's enterprise brought the first level and the first mill into being during the 18th century. I found a fireplace – an incongruous feature in a fragment of building – bearing the names of miners who had worked here some 150 years ago. Among the surnames were Cherry and Thornborrow.

Matthew Cherry has tales about almost every feature. His father, John, found a burial place among the stones. He was out ferreting when he removed some material at the base of the cliff, revealing the skeleton of a young man who had lived in ancient times. The corpse had been buried in a seated position, with stone flags round about.

Father returned to the spot with his friend Talbot Raw. As they worked to free the skeleton, Tal observed: "Nivver mind botherin' wi' them bones. Look for 'is purse".

Beyond a single-span, packhorse-type bridge which crosses a gorge, the gill closed in and was swaddled with the foliage of trees. Ahead, and first seen through a curtain of rowan leaves, I located Swinnergill Kirk. The song of a wren, which is normally loud, was especially so in the confines of the gill.

The cave, a miserable place, some 70 ft. in length, is said to have been the meeting place of local Nonconformists in a time of religious intolerance. Scouts were posted to give early warning of strangers. I felt sure that a "secret" meeting place somewhat handier to the homes of the people could have been found.

A moorland footpath connects Swinnergill with Gunnerside Gill. In spring, the cock grouse talk to each other, and not always in a friendly way. These birds are crowing from first to last light. They chase each other as they secure the space needed for nesting.

At daybreak, a moorcock [to use a common Pennine name] takes to the air in a dramatic song flight, calling *ka ka ka-ka-ka*. The bird is advertising for a mate. If successful, a hen bird flies into his territory. He must work hard to keep her. Neighbouring cock grouse do their best to entice or chase her into their territories.

Moorland conditions, well over 1,000 ft. above sea level, can be hard and ruthless. Some birds, weakened by disease, give up the struggle and their bodies are found in gutters. The hen grouse feeds voraciously on heather shoots and the tips of cotton-grass, building up condition for egg-laying.

The gamekeepers burn rank old heather to encourage new growth, food for grouse and sheep. Well-maintained moorland is good for the upland waders – for curlew, golden plover and dunlin. Our smallest falcon, the merlin, nests among the heather.

A red grouse population may be affected by disease, induced by the strongyle threadworm, a parasite which attacks the digestive tract, causing weakness, poor breeding performance or even death. Red grouse need to take in grit to help them to digest their tough moorland food. Ingeniously, the grit put out on the moors where natural grit is scarce is now medicated to reduce the ravages of the strongyle worm.

I strode in an area of fascinating names: Hungry Hushes, Botcher Gill and Sir Francis. Not the least fascinating aspect of lead-mining to students are the names of underground systems, recorded on old maps – Cock Rakes and Blind Gill, Priscilla and Brandy Bottle, Punchard and Hard Level.

Nowhere was I to detect such an eerie, leadmine-ish atmosphere as in Gunnerside Gill, where crumbling masonry, waste-heaps and the dank and dripping mouths of adits were monuments to t'deeard past. In the upper gill, heather-covered slopes sweep grandly to the edge of the beck. Water trickling down a cliff stimulates a lush growth of mosses.

The footpath I followed from Swinnergill is part of the Coast to Coast Walk devised by A. Wainwright, of Kendal. He did not find beauty in dereliction but confessed to finding the Lead Mining Country interesting.

Gunnerside Gill's lost-world appearance drew from me a strong emotional response. I saw a roofless, windowless, doorless building, on a ledge created by spoil from old mines, and was impelled to try, in my mind's eye, to provide the missing ingredient – people. Or to try and discover some of their secrets, such as how they managed to devise a mortar of astonishing toughness. Lime was the main ingredient, but was there something else? Could the "toughening" agent have been flue dust?

The main spectacle of the Gill is where the valley divides, forming a Y-shape. At the point of division is a rounded hill with limestone crags, the hill's face holds evidence of gruver's activity – in particular, a lime kiln. The smelt mill is now much decayed and the flue collapsed for nearly all its course. The chimney on the moortop was demolished.

Crossing the beck by what remains of a flagged bridge, I entered the roofless peat house, its arched doorways indicating where horse-drawn carts laden with peat were backed to provide a reserve of fuel for smelting.

Further down the gill, I re-located the compressor at Sir Francis Level, which was made for horses and is thus wider than most of the others in Gunnerside Gill. The big wheel and much ancillary equipment were removed and a subterranean engine house robbed of equipment and tools left there when the mine closed.

Attempts were made to salvage the compressor, but its enormous iron chamber, resembling an old and rusting submarine, lies there, still in a recognisable form. It is said to have been transporter here over Hardstiles, using the old road from Richmond and with a dozen horses as motive power. At Sir Francis Level, it was set to work to renew the fouled air deep in the mine and also to power the pneumatic drills.

So to Old Gang, reached by a moorland track, from which I once saw a large bird take off with something clasped between its thighs. It was a woodcock, carrying one of its young. I do not claim that woodcock habitually carry their young when danger threatens. I can only record that, with Matthew Cherry as a witness, I actually saw it happen. On the Pennines, the woodcock does not always lives up to its name. I have found nests on open fellsides.

Wainwright, the celebrated fell-walker, who had a feeling for words as well as being a meticulous artist, included Old Gang on his Coast to Coast route. He noted: "For a third of a mile not a blade of grass nor a sprig of heather is seen, the natural moorland having been transformed into an arid desert of stone".

I stopped for a chat with a man who was reclaiming minerals from spoil heaps. After that, I shared Old Gang only with the grouse, though perhaps the ghost of Old Curly still flits around this industrialised little valley. Curly was the subject of an oil painting of about 1750. He was depicted as an Old Gang Worthy, and it was possibly the earliest portrayal of a Yorkshire lead miner.

There must have been hundreds like him – men wearing heavy clogs, with strong woollen stockings and tight clothes, for there must be no "drag" in the constricted passages under-ground. Curly carried a horn lantern. In the background to the painting (all trace of the original has been lost) are ant-like figures on an old mining road.

Old Gang throve between the late 17th and late 19th centuries; its heyday being from 1830 to 1870. Here was a mining complex, with smelt mills, flues, a roasting furnace and blacksmith's shop. The coal used for many years was that mined on Tan Hill.

Twenty years after Old Curly was commemorated on a painting, the two brothers Spensely were killed "in Lead Mines at Old Gang", an early use of the name. They worked in the period of the old smelt mill, when people lived near their work. In 1744, as revealed

Hillside farm in Swaledale (Tom Sykes).

Barns near Langthwaite (John le Roy).

by the parish records, the christening took place of Mary, daughter of John Borrass, of "Level Houss, Old Gang".

A new mill was built about 1790 near the mouth of Hard Level, being part of the re-organisation of the industry by Lord Pomfret and Peter Denys. The mill flue, into which five smaller flues ran, extended without deviation to the foot of a crag some 2,250 ft. away; thence up the face of the crag to where a large chimney was built at an elevation of 1,820 ft., or over 500 ft. above the mill it served. Ore was delivered to Old Gang from rich workings associated with the Friarfold Vein complex.

A short climb up the hill brought me to the remains of a peat house – an astonishing building, 391 feet long, 21 ft. wide and, in its working days, thatched but left open-sided so that any stored peat might continue to dry under the influence of drying breezes.

The size of this enormous building was dictated by the necessity of having to cut all the peat in early summer. By late summer, a year's supply of peat was in storage.

I walked down the track in the company of grouse. They were in lively conversation. I tried to join in by simulating a run of becking calls – *kowa, kowa, kowa*. The grouse were not in the mood to be teased.

8

BOOZE
AND BEYOND

I enter Herriotshire and recall the James Herriot stories of a young vet in the Dales. I stride through a pub-less hamlet named Booze and see another tract of landscape where the lead-miners wiped their feet. The day ends on Fremington Edge, with a walk against a gale-force wind.

A rainbow arched itself over Arkengarthdale, where the Norseman Arkil had his farm. Before the end of the day, shafts of sunlight would draw attention to individual features in an austere but stunning countryside.

They would illuminate, for a minute or two at a time, a farmstead or field barn or a pasture hard-won from moorland which, elsewhere, was doing its best to cover up the scars of mining. I would see a pattern of walls, made from stones plucked from the locality and therefore blending with it.

The road from Surrender Bridge to Arkengarthdale was a strip of tarmac on an open moor until it entered a declivity and was over-run by a beck. This water-splash was made famous through its inclusion in the introductory sequence of the television series based on the Herriot books.

For umpteen years, millions of television viewers warmed to stories of a young vet who worked in the Yorkshire Dales while the Dales were as yet throughly "local" and full of characters. A jingly tune accompanied the start of each episode and we saw the vet's cart bouncing over Langthwaite Bridge and then splashing through the beck on the moorland road.

This was now my point of entry into Herriotshire, where guide books and catering places bear the name Herriot. The vet had, through books and subsequently films, shared his great love of the Dales with millions of people.

On qualifying in Glasgow, during the job-scarce years of the 1930s, James Herriot joined a practice at Thirsk. Part of his work was helping the vet at Leyburn and thus he became familiar with the Dales.

It was at the tail-end of a long tradition – a time when horses were common, butter or cheese were made from the milk of Shorthorn cattle and there was a touch of black-magic in the remedies for ailing stock which, today, are cured instantly by the jab of a syringe.

Herriot was happy dealing with the dalesfolk, who before the introduction of radio and television, also improved transport and a shifting of populations, sustained the old fellside life which had been built up through centuries of isolation. The dalesfolk were somewhat brusque but genuine.

The Herriot books, and the films made from them, have spread his account of old-time Dales life into every part of the world. We were introduced to Helen, James's girl friend and subsequently his wife. We warmed to Tristran, Farnon's wayward younger brother, and to a fine "supporting cast".

I once asked a Dales farmer about the way of life in the 1930s and he replied: "Thee read 'erriot!"

I was striding through Herriot Country. Arkengarthdale, the most northerly parish in the

Booze, Arkengarthdale.

Springtime, near Booze.

Yorkshire Dales National Park, was to be seen dimly through a curtain of rain. The Weather Clerk had a headache. There was little point in looking for sunshine that morning for, as an old friend says of Dales weather – "it could do owt!"

The dales country was being rain-washed and a landscape which had been picked over by miners looked more careworn than ever. I passed spoil heaps and crumbling masonry indicating yet another haunt of t'auld man.

I cheered up at CB, the only place in England where the name is composed of initials – or so I have been told. They represent Charles Bathurst, grandson to Dr. John, the physician to Oliver Cromwell. Charles bought the manor of Arkengarthdale in 1656 and developed the lead mines.

Bob Carter, who lived round the corner from the CB Inn and just across the road from a field holding an octagonal gunpowder store associated with the lead-mining, was my main source of local information.

He told me that the dale once had five inns, including "The Jolly Dogs" and the "Lily Jock", which was visited by Sir Walter Scott and had an associated miners' club. In addition, there were four beer-houses. Mining was a dry job. The urge to imbibe was discouraged by the Methodists, who then built an enormous chapel.

Harking back to the miners' club, Bob told me that for a Club Walk the men wore off-white fustian trousers, coats with tails [known locally as clay-hammer jackets] and cravats in which "Lily Jock" pins were stuck. The miners had their Mechanics' Institute at CB Terrace and smallholders with livestock banded together in a Cow Club.

Bob's grandfather had been mine agent and "a lot o' fore-elders" were miners. Uncle John Hutchinson began work at the age of eight and held candles for miners. He graduated to operating the "windy king", which was designed to send a current of air into the workings. "At Stand Mine," said Bob, "a man could burn out a whole tallow candle before he reached t'spot where he was working".

Before the last of the local lead mines closed in 1912, the sound of clogs rang incessantly through the dale. The women of Langthwaite and Booze – repeat, Booze! – had clogs on their feet as they walked to the workings at Old Gang.

The women knitted stockings as they strode along, for the mine-owner paid only a shilling for a 12-hour day. The income was augmented by selling knitted goods. Old Ruth, of Langthwaite, who lived at the turn of the present century, carried food in a red and white handkerchief. She ate her meal in the blacksmith's shop.

The thunderous roar of clogs became just a clatter when the mines had closed. Now, it was mainly the farmers who wore them, though schoolchildren had tiny clogs on their feet as they went to school. The boys slurred their feet, trying to raise sparks from the clog-irons, which were known as "caulkers".

Yet another storm swept the dale. I took sanctuary in the Anglican church, a novel example (in the Dales) of a "Commissioners' church", constructed after Waterloo, mainly from cash which was advanced by Parliament.

Arkengarthdale is not short of roads and tracks. A road from Reeth passes through the dale and then crosses high land at Tan Hill, where stand the highest licensed premises in England. The main road through Arkengarthdale is unfenced at both ends. Sheep – of the Swaledale breed, of course – are at liberty to cross. A road beginning near the celebrated CB Inn traverses the Stang Pass to Barnard Castle.

I walked the short distance to Langthwaite, passing the Methodist chapel and marvelling at the faith – and number of chapelgoers – needed to sustain such a huge edifice. During

Looking across Arkengarthdale (M. Templeman).

Bridge and cottages at Langthwaite.

On the edge of Reeth (Den Oldroyd).

the heyday of Nonconformity, the Established Church did little more than tick-over. The Methodists were more widely represented. Meeting places for worship were opened in many places, even at a tiny settlement like Whaw. At Booze, members met in private houses.

Early last century, the Arkengarthdale curate bemoaned the fact that "the methodists, finding that I gather the people to the church, now keep themselves entirely from it and oppose me with all their might".

In turn, the Wesleyans were upset when the Primitive Methodists, having broken away from the main flock in 1812, began to witness in the Dales, with fervent worship and lusty outdoor "camp" meetings. They also despatched travelling preachers to the remoter areas, even to Booze, where in 1831 the local "Prims" were admonished for not contributing enough cash towards travelling expenses.

Methodism had its ups and downs, having a spiritual resurgence in the late 1830s and later in the century. On a preaching plan for the Wesleyan Circuit based on Reeth (1851) appear the names of meeting places at Marske, Marrick, Hurst, Reeth, Healaugh, High and Low Whita, Low Row, Gunnerside, Calvert Houses, Muker, Keld, Arkle Town, Whaw and William Gill. The average attendance on a specific Sunday in March that year was 1,400 adults.

In its more fervent days, worshippers punctuated a sermon with loud "Amens" and "Hallelujahs". It is said that at a revival meeting, a woman was so moved she prayed: "Oh, Lord, tak our Jack and ho'd 'im by his clogs ower Hell Fire". Then, remembering the clogs were new, and not wanting them to be scorched, she added: "But nobbut give him a swither".

Methodism, which throve in the lead-mining areas, went into a fairly rapid decline when the mines closed and the mining families dispersed. It was left to the old farming families to support the chapels and now, with smaller family units, emigration of young people and a decline in church-going, many a rural chapel has only a handful of members.

Dalesfolk are by and large law-abiding. When I met PC Dick Cresswell, who from a base at Reeth was given the task of policing 88,000 acres of moor and dale that comprise the largest beat for a single officer in England, he told me that he had far more trouble from the "poaching" fraternity than the natives.

The poachers were mainly from the north-east towns who, driving "old bangers" and having nets or lamps and lurchers, turned off the Great North Road at Scotch Corner and passed through Richmond to go rabbiting in the dale.

Said Dick: "The so-called poachers are not very proficient. I know there are a lot of rabbits about, but they don't catch very many." He had watched these unwelcome visitors for hours. They were not really poaching as he would define the term. He described them as "rural vandals".

One Sunday morning, he was called to Marrick, where two farmers had blocked in a car suspected of being used by poachers. There was a tractor at one side and a Land Rover at the other. Dick looked into the car and saw a ferret box on the back seat.

A chap came walking up. He had nothing with him. Dick asked him if it was his car, and he said it was. "Have you been doing a spot of poaching?" "No". "What are you doing with a ferret box in the back of your car?" He said: "You can't catch rabbits with a ferret box".

One of the farm lads had a hunch where the man had been. The man said he was alone but a suspicious-looking man was standing on the road, looking over the wall. Dick drove towards him, wound down the window of his car and said: "Your mate wants you back at his car". "Oh – all right," he replied, to Dick's quiet satisfaction. He told the two men: "You'd best be out of the parish."

I stood on the bridge at Langthwaite and stared down at the beck which is normally well-mannered but quickly responds to excessive rain on the fells. Dick Cresswell had mentioned extensive flooding during which a rescue helicopter was called out.

The shopkeeper recalled his years spent at the quert workings which are on the hill at an elevation of 1,100 ft. Chert, a hard, flint-like stone, was once quarried and, as the reserves were depleted, abstracted from underground workings, where within living memory men worked by candlelight in a constant temperature of about 45 degrees fahrenheit.

A farmer arrived from the hilltop hamlet of Booze with a Land Rover and trailer containing milk from his cattle which was kept refrigerated until the milk lorry arrived.

Booze? What's in a name? A local man had "heard tell" it came from *bouse*, a lead-mining term. I'd also heard it was from the Old English *boga-hus*, meaning "a house by the bow or curve". Years ago, the postman told me the name came from "the house on the bow of the hill". He invited me to say "bow-house" quickly a few times and then add a Dales intonation. I found myself uttering the word "booze"!

The hamlet stands on a hill-end, some 600 feet above Arkle Beck. A few farms and cottages catch the eye of the sun and are battered by winter gales. There is but one motor road, which is steep, constricted and winding. In spring, the verges are festooned by flowers and at Booze itself the floral display is breathtaking. Waste ground is bright with yellow mountain pansies and patches of the lead-mining plant, spring sandwort, are easily found.

As the road reaches the edge of Booze, the tarmac peters out, to be succeeded by a rough track, the centre of which is tufty with grass. The hamlet has no inn, no shop, no chapel. A.J. Brown wrote: "Booze, despite its encouraging name, is about the most teetotal hamlet I have every explored, hopefully, from end to bitter end".

Down by the Arkle Beck is the entrance to Booze Wood level, which was driven north-wards to encounter the profitable Booze Vein. It is said that the lead-mining was so profitable that 32 families lived at the hamlet. An old man I met 20 years ago told me that when he was a schoolboy he saw the few remaining miners go clatteringly to work, wearing clogs. He also saw miners carry lead, in small bags, to a collecting point at the CB Inn.

A farmer remembered the butter-making days and how butter was taken to the shop in Langthwaite, for onward transit to Richmond. The surplus farm stock was sold at Barney [Barnard Castle]. He remembered driving two good cows along the 10 mile route to the town in 1928, when the cows sold for £49. There was not much brass to be earned at Booze. "Living's all reet," he said, "it's getting a living that's main worry".

In inconspicuous path led from Booze into Slei Gill, which was served by a miner's road – a route that linked the mines and narrowed on its way to Booze Moor, sharing a small gap with a waterfall.

Names on the map reflect the twin occupations of sheep-farming and lead-mining. Hunger House is a sheepfold. North Rake Hush marks one of those places where mineral veins were exposed by a rush of water from a dam. The map is littered by marks signifying disused shafts.

The wind moaned across a sheep-weary, man-despoiled landscape. Mostly, it was cloudy. Occasionally there were shafts of sunlight, to pick out features such as field barns, walls and the grassed-over craters of old bell-pits.

On Fremington Edge, rain was hurled at me by a stiff wind. The sheep snuggled in the lee of the wall which runs for a mile or two a little way back from the Edge itself. A golden plover looked storm-shocked.

Anglian settlements were the beginnings of various local settlements, with Fremington as "the farmstead of Fram's people" and Reeth being named in relation to the beck. Grinton,

Mining country, near Booze.

Mine-weary landscape, near Fremington Edge.

the village near Reeth which has the parish church, was simply "the green enclosure".

A track down an easy part of the limestone scar to High Fremington led me close to some old chert workings. Here, when the chert had been hacked out of the beds by hand, it was trimmed to a handy size and transported by lorry to the potteries at Richmond, where it was ground into a powder for the manufacture of china-ware.

At Reeth, which I approached through meadows, Georgian houses, chapels and inns were keeping an eye on each other across a spacious green. A former Methodist schoolroom is now the Swaledale Folk Museum. At a cafe, I heard of the man who provided a special service on the Coast to Coast route, transporting the kit of walkers from one bed and breakfast establishment to another so that they might travel light.

Reeth reminded me of my chat with Dick Cresswell, the bobby, and his account of what happened when Arkle Beck overflowed one night.

Dick, having acquired some pheasant eggs from a friend, hatched them out and, on a sunny Bank Holiday Monday, put the poults in a cage on the lawn, where they cheeped happily all day. Rain began to fall during the night. "We awoke, hearing a hissing sound... I heard the young pheasants cheeping. I looked out and saw water filling the garden. One or two birds had drowned."

Gradually, the enormity of the flooding became apparent. A 999 call was received and he set off for Langthwaite, where two people were leaning from an upper window of the local inn. The beck had overflowed and the water was so deep Dick advised them to stay upstairs.

He returned to Reeth, where he had to wade for the last stretch to the police house. He climbed into the house through a window. His wife reported that when she came downstairs, conditions did not seem to be so bad until she stepped on to a carpet – which was floating! The fire brigade was dealing with flooding at the vicarage.

A camp and caravan park had gone under water, and fortunately no lives were lost. Soon a helicopter was buzzing overhead. The Memorial Hall was opened to receive the cold and wet holidaymakers.

Dick had told his tale as we stood at the edge of the moor above Grinton, looking out over Reeth, and seeing the convergence of Swaledale and Arkengarthdale. It was a splendid view of dale and fell, village and farm, ribbed by drystone walls.

When the constable had driven off, I looked down the valley of the Swale towards Richmond. It was while motoring over Bellerby Moor, from Leyburn to Grinton, that James Herriot was first struck by the "magic" of the Dales.

He had stopped his car to let out the dog. He sat down and looked about him. "I felt as though I had suddenly been transported to a magical land," he was to recall.

I had asked James Herriot about his Dales jaunts, knowing that his home was in Thirsk, which lies between the Dales and the Hambleton Hills. He explained: "We had a partner called Frank Bingham, a famous vet in Leyburn. (I called him Ewan Ross in my books)."

Frank Bingham was a tall, handsome Irishman. "Like a lot of the vets in those days, he liked a drink. Many apocryphal tales are told about him. But he was a wonderful chap, one of my favourite men. He was very kind to me."

On three days a week, James Herriot set off from Thirsk to Leyburn at 6 a.m., returning home on the same day. He travelled about the Dales in "a funny old Austin 10." All vets were impecunious in every way. "This car had no heater, of course. The floor was broken and every time I went over a puddle the muddy water would splash up into my face. The windscreen was cracked and there were only one or two places I could peer through.

"Amazingly, it took me on my rounds, up hill and down dale. There was one terrible period when the brakes did not work. We couldn't get around to sorting out the brakes, so I drove all over the hilly places without being able to use them.

"I put a bit in my book about travelling into West Witton from the moortop and negotiating that terrible hairpin bend without any brakes on the car". He paused and added: "I wouldn't do that now if you gave me a million pounds . . . But then, I was young and tireless".

9

AYSGARTH FALLS
AND SEMERWATER

I watch red grouse in Apedale and at Bolton Castle tour a medieval apartment-block. Aysgarth offers me a spectacle of tumbling water. I walk round Semerwater, looking for a "drowned city" and follow the Stake Pass to upper Wharfedale.

Springtime was arriving in the Dales villages with a profusion of golden daffodils – lanky daffodils, more vulnerable to a sneaky easterly wind than the little wild sort which the Wordsworths saw in Glencoyne Wood, on the shores of Ullswater.

Spring had yet to capture the Pennine heights. There was a chill in the air as I followed the high road from Grinton to Askrigg – a road passing disused mine shafts and tips. At Ridley Hush, to the north of Greets Moss and Coal Pit Moor, I thankfully left the tarmac for a strip of beaten earth. It was a route which took me directly to the mouth of Apedale. Looking at the name on the map, I felt to be on safari.

The moor held tetchy [irritable] moorcock and grouse butts, also a profusion of old mine workings. My map indicated that, away to the east, on and beyond Redmire Moor, the ground was riddled with bell-pits which were sunk to reach seams of coal.

When I turned into Apedale I glanced at the map and noticed – with a chill of horror – an eminence called Gibbon Hill!

Apedale Beck receives transfusions of cold water by way of Sour Gill and Black Gutter, South Grain and Smithy Gill. The runnels are represented on the map by thin blue lines which resemble the the pattern of veins on the back of a leaf.

I can assure any timid readers that no apes wander in Apedale, this green fingerprint on the purple of the high moors. Apedale derives its name from a Norseman called Api. Miners ransacked Apedale for its mineral wealth, leaving much evidence of their activity. They rent the hills with "hushes". They left unsightly spoil heaps.

Sheep, the unofficial green-keepers of the Dales, keep the vegetation trimmed. At Apedale Head, I reached an outpost of civilisation as indicated by a wheelless railway goods van, now used as an outbarn, holding food for wintering sheep.

Apedale appears to suit grouse, judging by their number and condition. Grouse-spotting was easy from the track. In early spring, the males were showing aggression to each other, keen to hold territory and any attendant female. The plumage of a grouse is a glorious russet tone. Red wattles are inflated during territorial disputes. The eyes of the cock grouse are large, ringed with white. The bill, though small, is strong enough to deal with tough moorland fare.

In March, a hen grouse is pursued by a cock bird which is desperate to keep her in his territory. There is territorial pressure from other cock birds all around. Disputes flare up. The moorland air shivers with the crowing and clucking of amorous birds.

The hens, when sitting on their large clutches of eggs, rely on stillness and their cryptic colouration to avoid detection by predators. Each bird incubates for hours on end, covering the eggs like a feathered tea-cosy. Several times a day, a hen bird slips off her nest to feed, drink and defecate, leaving an extra-large dropping which is known as a "clocking foil".

The broad green floor of Wensleydale.

A flock of sheep near Castle Bolton.

The cock grouse is the sentry, providing warning of the approach of enemies, mainly foxes and carrion crows. Grouse chicks are alert and active almost from the point of hatching. They stay near the nest for a while; then they are led to the areas of moor which are damp and mossy – a source of protein-rich insect food. The precocious chicks feed voraciously and, even when their wings seem little more than stumps, surprise any intruder by taking off – whirring through the air on short-lived flights.

A rich insect diet sustains the chicks. As young adults, they dine on the heather shoots. Having a specialised gut, the red grouse takes some grit into the large gizzard as a grinding agent, using the grit to break down the fibrous diet of heather.

By the end of the nesting season, the moor holds family parties of grouse. In early August, these are subjected to a hail of shot from "sportsmen" in the butts. It has been estimated that a driven bird attains a speed of 60 miles an hour as it zips low over the ground.

So much for the grouse. My walk took me to the point where I had to select a new path. Rather than going directly to Castle Bolton, which is the most popular route, I walked on to Redmire, hoping to see the arrival of a daily mineral train bringing empty hoppers to be filled with ground limestone. After some clever shunting, the locomotive returns eastwards with a load for industrial use at Redcar.

In the days of regular steam, I knew the Wensleydale line well. I would disembark from the Settle-Carlisle at Garsdale and clamber on to a short stopping train for Hawes and points east. Once, being the only passenger, I was allowed to travel on the footplate!

The line was closed west of Redmire, but to the east the track was needed for lime-trains, which made a slow, somewhat tedious way up the dale, all but the driver being engaged in opening and closing the many gates. This is why a modern locomotive and trucks tows a 40-year-old guards van. With a guard installed, the gate duties can be speeded up.

I came to an area where lime dust from the quarry gave a perpetual wintry appearance to the trees round about. On the road down the hill my boots disturbed fine lime dust. A heavily-laden lorry swung off it and ground its way towards the old station. Soon the lorry had reversed to the edge of an enormous hopper; the back of the vehicle was raised and a gravitation pull did the rest. Pulverised rock descended into the hopper. From here, the limestone was deposited into the mini-hoppers of the railway train.

With the lines on an impressive gradient, any shunting could be done by hand. A man, with two trucks, walked along, controlling their movement by handbrake. When the hoppers were full, the brakes were released and they moved slowly to the sidings from which they would be collected by train.

The train arrived at 12-40. It was impressively modern – and very long. I had not been expecting anything quite as large and powerful as the Class 60 diesel locomotive, the largest used with freight traffic. The driver, who had driven locomotives up the Wensleydale line in the age of steam, used great precision in moving about the hopper waggons in a constricted area.

He gave me a personalised toot on the klaxon as he drew out of Redmire on his return trip with some 1,800 tons of lime for the steelworks.

It was Fred Lawson, the artist, who introduced me to the natural beauty of the Castle Bolton district. Fred liked the moor edges – the "scraggy bits, with a few trees". He had first visited Castle Bolton for a short holiday at the invitation of an artist friend. It became his home for the rest of his life. He married a daleswoman, Muriel Metcalfe, and both she and their daughter Sonia have also achieved renown as artists.

To Fred, not having a car was an advantage, for after a short walk he had to sit down and paint something. His motoring friends, travelling up hill, down dale, were still looking for good subjects when the sun began to set!

Fred had drawn or painted Bolton Castle from every angle except looking downwards. He knew every crack and cranny and pointed out to me a hollow wall in which a local lady kept her pig overnight. She allowed the pig to enter head-first and had great difficult in recovering it next morning. Henceforth, the pig was backed into the wall cavity.

Fred wrote and illustrated a monthly letter for "The Dalesman". One month, when it had not arrived, I rang up the postmistress at Bolton (Fred did not have a telephone) and mentioned the dilemma. She said: "I thought that Fred hadn't posted it to you this month." I was told that I should not worry. When he came in, she would get him to sit down and write the letter and make a sketch. These would then be posted to me.

The flag of St George was flying above Bolton Castle, where the young owner, Harry Orde-Powlett, had been instilling new life into this fortified house. When I met him at its re-launch as a Dales tourist attraction, he confessed that he would like to see a pennant featuring some Scrope family heraldry, including perhaps an assembly of Cornish choughs!

Bolton Castle stands on a rock ledge where, in ancient times, the indigenous Forest of Wensleydale gave way to open ground. My Lords Scrope (pronounce their name Scroop) wanted a castle with a view and they got it. Across the dale lies Pen Hill, its slopes a series of bold horizontals caused by the Yoredale strata.

Unlike the popular idea of a Castle, with moat and drawbridge, Bolton was built as a block of palatial flats within one defensive structure. Towards the end of last century, the place had degenerated into a partly-ruined tenement occupied by labourers and their families. Then, about the turn of the century, Lord Bolton took the place in hand and consolidated what remained. The stern old castle shows its best side, with few signs of ruin, to those who approach it from the dale.

Mary, Queen of Scots, languished here in the days of the first Elizabeth. For six months, from July to January, she was held captive in Wensleydale, awaiting the Queen's pleasure. She occupied Lord Scrope's private apartments – rooms that mirrored her high rank – and presumably she also took over Scrope's bedchamber at the top of the tower.

Scrope and Sir Francis Knollys, who had been her co-gaolers while at Carlisle, were continually writing letters to the Queen or Sir William Cecil in London asking what they should do in certain circumstances, such as if the Queen desired to return to Scotland. At Bolton they treated her well. Her stay cost them dearly, the distinguished visitor and her retainers – all with hearty appetites – outnumbering the men of the garrison.

Mary, Queen of Scots, is represented in the modern Bolton Castle by an authentically-clad dummy.

Using paths across large fields, I headed westwards to Aysgarth. At Carperby, I visited "The Wheatsheaf", the hostelry where the newly-wed Mr. and Mrs. Alf Wight (James Herriot and his missus) spent their honeymoon, a venue chosen because Alf had had agreed to combine his honeymoon with urgent veterinary work.

At Freeholders' Wood, a 27-acre hazel coppice, I was in one part of Wensleydale that had changed little in appearance since medieval times. The boom of falling water directed me to Aysgarth Falls.

The Ure, having cut through soft layers of shale to expose the upper beds of the Limestone, makes a boisterous descent of about 100 ft in a mile and a-half. It tumbles from ledges of rock at a trio of grand cascades. One dalesman I met wondered what all the fuss was about, adding: "They're nobbut rock and watter!"

Bolton Castle (Fred Lawson).

Aysgarth Falls (Karl Stedman).

To Bishop Pococke, in the mid-18th century, they were comparable with the cataracts of the Nile. A local poet named Maud turned out a vivid couplet:

Till probe again, with tumult's wildest roar,
Recoils the billows, rocks the giddy shore.

Pennant wrote of "the gloom of the pendant trees, the towering steeple of the church above, and the range of the waters beneath the ivy-bound arch." That arch is a bridge crossing the Ure in a single 70 ft span. Turner, as a young artist, made pencil sketches for one of his "Richmondshire" studies – a picture he eventually sold for £5.

Touriod pressure is acute. No longer is it possible to park the car near the bridge in order to take a photograph. A delay of 10 seconds results in a traffic snarl-up. Yellow lines were painted at the roadside as long ago as the summer of 1975 and they discourage dawdling.

Having joined the ice cream brigade on the bridge, I saw the upper falls tumbling from broad shallow terraces of rock with a pleasingly orderly appearance. The middle falls, when viewed from the Carperby bank, could be admired in relation to Aysgarth Church, the place of workship that appealed to Pennant.

The lower falls, approached by a footpath in a woodland setting, were over a mile from the upper falls and marked not only the end of this stretch of turbulent water but also the end of the upper dale and the River Ure's entry into a park-like countryside.

A footpath north of the river led me to a river crossing at Worton, from which I used field paths to Bainbridge. The village is named after the River Bain, some two miles long, and said to be the "shortest river in England". Brough Hill, an eminence near the river, was the site of a Roman fort, part of a system by which the Romans policed the land of the Brigantes.

For me, a glimpse of Bainbridge recalls Dick Chapman, a Wensleydale lad who became a schoolteacher in Bradford. He returned to the dale for a long and contented retirement. I watched Dick catch crayfish by dangling bait in the river while leaning over his garden wall. I saw him puffing his pipe and yarning with his pals in the bar of the "Rose and Crown". He showed me a Bronze Age spearhead picked up on the shores of Semerwater.

Dick was friendly with J. B. Priestley and tried to teach the distinguished writer how to catch crayfish. On a visit to the dale during which "Jack" Priestley collected impressions for an article to appear in an American magazine, he stayed at the "Rose and Crown". It was here I arranged to meet him for an interview.

As I approached the main door, I heard the tapping of typewriter keys and from a partly opened bedroom window saw the appearance of grey wraiths of pipe smoke. Priestley, when working, was surrounded by as much smoke as a factory chimney in his native Bradford.

I kept close to the River Bain on my walk to Semerwater, trying to remember "The Ballad of Semerwater", a poem by William Watson which tells of a city overwhelmed by water because of its inhospitality to a begger man. It begins:

Deep asleep, deep asleep,
Deep asleep it lies -
The still lake of Semerwater...

Dick Chapman, who had known the lake since his youth, once swam across it with his brother. They had stripped naked and intended to come ashore at a large limestone boulder called The Carlow Stone. Here they would rest in the sunshine before swimming back to their clothes.

As they neared the Carlow Stone, they became aware of an assembly of people and the singing of a hymn. A religious service was being held. They had to stand neck-deep in water, recovering their breath, before returning to where their adventure had begun.

Dick mentioned the presence of a causeway extending into Semerwater from near the Carlow Stone. He also told me of evidence of an Iron Age lake dwelling place. Did the old story of the "drowned city" begin when people heard of an old lake settlement being overwhelmed by one of Semerwater's celebrated flash-floods?

Once a year, in summer, Semerwater has a floating pulpit. An outdoor service takes place. For an hour, the motor boats which draw water-skiers across the shallow lake are silent. The cleric of Stalling Busk (who also has the supervision of the large Askrigg parish) is carried out to a boat and stands there to lead the service, his congregation sitting on chairs lined up on the pebbly shore.

The vicar announces hymns, which are accompanied by the Hawes Band. He leads the prayers, has a short address and after pronouncing the Benediction remarks: "I cannot, alas, walk on water..." Whereupon a man who has taken off his shoes and stockings gives him a piggy-back ride back to the shore.

I walked round Semerwater, seeing a flotilla of Canada geese and assorted ducks. The ruined church of Stalling Busk could be viewed by leaning over a wall. I had a chat with the Ewbanks of Marsett about Methodist occasions past and present.

The Stake Pass, part of the old Roman road from Bainbridge to Ilkley, was my route to Wharfedale. I walked from Stalling Busk, between Stake Allotments and Cragdale Moor, turning south to cross Stake Moss on my way to Kidstones Pass, which lies between Bishopdale and Wharfedale.

At the highest point of the Stake (1,836 ft) I felt that I did not walk alone. This is an ancient route. If there is a ghost on the Stake it will probably be that of a woman travelling by spectral horse-litter with ghostly attendants – Lady Anne Clifford, crossing from her Skipton estate to that of Westmorland. She stayed with kinsfolk in Wensleydale before continuing by another hilltop route to Mallerstang.

Born in Skipton, in 1590, Lady Anne was twice married and could recall the reigns of Queen Elizabeth, James I, Charles I, Cromwell and Charles II. Though she spent much of her life in the south, Lady Anne fought for her northern inheritance, which had passed to another.

When she came into her own, just after the Civil War, she set about restoring her family property, cheerfully ignoring Cromwell's desire that "slighted" castles should remain slighted.

She made an almost Royal progress about the countryside and was familiar with the route "upp Buckden Rakes and over the Staks into Wensleydale." Vita Sackville-West, in her introduction to Lady Anne's diary, suggests that most of us are born for some indicated function in life, although we may never have the good fortune to fulfil it. So was Lady Anne born to matriarchy.

Vita continued: "... and so I think I may safely say without too great a stretch of the misleading imagination of the biographer that it was not until she had passed her middle age that she entered into her true province. She was not born to be a wife and a young mother; she was born to be a great grandmother and a widow and so she continued active to the last."

Lady Anne's last years were spent "travelling over rough roads in all sorts of weathers between Skipton, Barden, Pendragon, Brough, Brougham and Appleby and she died finally

Rooftops at Askrigg (D. Dakeyne).

Semerwater (Janet Rawlins).

at the age of 86 in the room in Brougham Castle where her father had been born and her mother had died."

The Stake route was a favourite with cattle-drovers. Turner, visiting the Dales to sketch during the summer of 1816 had ever reason to remember the Stake crossing.

That summer was extremely wet.

10

UPPER WHARFEDALE
AND LITTONDALE

I pay my respects to Pastor Lindley, as represented in stained glass at Hubberholme Church, and I follow the course he regularly took over the Horse Head Pass to Halton Gill. After traversing Littondale, I enjoy a hilltop walk from Kettlewell and on the moor at Yarnbury see a smelt-mill chimney and recall when Paramount Pictures crowned the hilltop with a board and plaster representation of "Wuthering Heights".

Kidstones Pass took a leisurely, winding way into Wharfedale but the local becks were in a hurry, leaping from scar to scar. A recent storm had brought a responsive chorus from a dozen waterfalls. Major Horner, who was innkeeper/farmer at "The White Lion", Cray, used to say that the inn got its name from the white water and lusty roar of the ᴜ ᴄk.

Major (a Christian name, not a military title) was one of the last of his kind. When he took over at Cray, the pub was primarily a farmhouse with a licence for the sale of liquor. After drawing pints of ale in the bar, he hand-milked cattle in an adjacent shippon.

I strode down into a dale where glaciers had taken deep bites from the landscape. Both Bishopdale and Upper Wharfedale were gouged deeply in Pleistocene times.

The map shows the contour lines packed closely together. It also indicates that the head of Wharfedale, far from being austere, is well-wooded. Remnants of old forest cling to the sides, thriving in gills which are little visited.

The Dales National Park had completed the first stage of a survey of semi-natural Dales woods, which account for less than one per cent of the land surface of the Park but are the valued haunt of green woodpecker, tree creeper and nuthatch. The ground is generously spread with flowering plants.

The National Park surveyors dealt with three main categories of broad-leaved woods — ash wood, with an understorey of hazel and bird cherry, such as is common in limestone areas; the oak wood on deeper soils, and thirdly, low-lying woodland dominated by the damp-loving alder.

Many woods were found to be in poor shape and unlikely to retain their tree cover through the next century. Woods were found to be "slowly dying on their feet" because of unrestricted access by sheep and rabbits. As if that was not enough, over half the woods studied had signs of Dutch elm disease.

Buckden, the valley of the deer [a reference to Langstrothdale Chase], perpetuates the old associations. For centuries, red deer lay up by day and emerged from cover at half-light to browse in the woodland or to graze in the fields. A few red deer were seen hereabouts in the late 18th century.

The Misses Stansfield, of Buckden House, kept the old forest days alive with their stock of fallow deer. Miss Crompton Stansfield is recalled as an old lady, travelling along the snowbound road in a horse-drawn sleigh, driven by Old Baldock, her coachman. Major Horner had a spade-shaped antler from one of the last of the fallow bucks.

The roe, a non-herding species of deer, and a worthy quarry in the days of the Percies and Cliffords, has returned to the Pennine Dales, spreading southwards from the big Border conifer forests.

A roebuck in his foxy-red summer coat looks a splendid animal. In winter, he is clad in charcoal-grey. When alarmed, the roe gives a hoarse bark. The doe drops her twins in summer and promptly mates again, delayed implantation of the eggs in the womb ensuring that the young of the following year are born when the countryside has abundant food to sustain them.

I was now within sight of the Wharfe. When Fred Falshaw was a postman, he had to ford the river to deliver letters to a particular farm. I was told that when there was a spate, the farmer and Fred were standing on either side of the river. Fred fastened a postcard to a stone and hurled it across. The stone arrived at the foot of the farmer but the postcard fell into the river and was washed away. "Nivver mind, Fred," said the farmer, and – presuming that the postman had read the message on the card – he added: "What was on't?"

The Wharfe begins at Beckermonds with a merging of the Greenfield and Oughtershaw Becks. It flows under a high single-span bridge at Yockenthwaite, near which is what is claimed to be the finest Bronze Age stone circle in Wharfedale. Or the circle of stones may be what remains of a burial place.

Yockenthwaite was pronounced Yockinwit by the old-time farmers, one of whom was asked by a bemused visitor if he would spell it. The farmer thought and thought again before replying: "It isn't meant to be spelt – just said!"

I walked in from Buckden, along a straight road which goes under water in rainy spells. Soon, the two most venerable buildings in Hubberholme were in sight – the church across the river and the inn on the near side, with a substantial bridge in between.

Hubberholme Church was originally a forest chapel, built on an Anglo-Norse burial site and dedicated to St. Michael, who was usually called upon when a site had strong heathen associations. The walls are unplastered and an oaken rood loft of 1558 is still in place, though it should have been destroyed at the time of the Reformation, when an edict to that effect went out from York to the parishes.

I entered a building which contains mice – wooden mice, carved on the pews, the trademark of Thompson of Kilburn. They have adorned this church since 1934. I found a squirrel, dipper and Swaledale sheep among the creatures painted on glass by Francis Skeat and forming part of a stained glass window installed in 1970 in memory of the Robinson family.

The district still has a light cover of trees. A tract of woodland on the limestone scars above Hubberholme which had not been tidied up became a haunt of green woodpeckers. Many years ago, I was allowed to use a "hide" rigged up by a friend to photograph a pair.

Stan Lythe, who was handy with his hands, built a "pylon" hide of bits of wood taken from a Kettlewell cottage which was being restored. Said Stan: "I hope the woodpecker doesn't attack it. That wood is full of woodworm!"

Give a chance, nature does well by the upper Wharfe. Across at Kirkgill, a birch wood has sprung up naturally from an area where conifers were clear-felled in 1945.

The "George" inn at Hubberholme once belonged to the benefice, the same key unlocking inn and church. Someone painted on the doors of the toilets "Tups" (for gents) and "Yows" (for women).

Was the inn really a vicarage, as some people suppose? It is doubtful. There is no convenient historical slot in which the vicarage theory fits. Until the Reformation, the monks of Coverham took the service. Then the Perpetual Curate of Halton Gill officiated until Hubberholme became a parish in its own right in 1765. What served as the vicarage for many years was a conversion (in the late 19th century) of three miners' cottages.

Yockenthwaite, in Langstrothdale.

High pond near Conistone, Wharfedale.

The old link between kirk and inn is maintained annually when the Land Letting takes place, the land in question being the 16 acres of the Poor Pasture, available to the highest bidder. The ceremony takes place shortly after the New Year.

The vicar and his wardens form the House of Lords. The potential bidders are the House of Commons. There is much chatter, much banter, before a bid is accepted for the following 12 months.

A time limit is set on the ceremony by lighting an ordinary domestic candle. When the candle goes out, no more bids are accepted. The vicar startled one gathering by lighting one of the largest of ecclesiastical candles. But it was only a joke; he soon replaced it with one that would burn out in an hour or two.

The rent received for the Poor Pasture has traditionally been distributed among the poor of the parish. Now it is used to buy bags of coal for old-age pensioners at Christmas.

Back in the church, I again stood before the Robinson Window, delighted that it had survived a particularly low run by a jet aircraft which had caused much damage to local ceilings and windows. On the Window, I saw a representation of Thomas Lindley, curate of Halton Gill, riding a white horse through snow over the Horse Head Pass, as he would have been when travelling to a service at Hubberholme in winter.

Lindley was one of the best-known of the curates who served the two churches between 1807 and 1833. It is related that when the wardens at Hubberholme saw man and horse "break" the skyline, they rang the bell to summon people to attend.

I followed Pastor Lindley's route over Horse Head Moor, tramping along a series of zig-zags, trudging by Hag Beck, crossing the skyline and seeing, westwards, a stunning view of Penyghent with Penyghent Gill looking mysterious because it was in deep shadow.

The head of the pass is just 50 ft short of the 2,000 ft necessary for mountainhood. At Halton Gill I turned down the dale, keeping as close as I could to the river and hearing the "kleep" of oystercatchers, which nest on the shingle and in the adjacent fields.

A river path led me down to Arncliffe, which unlike the other settlements lies on the south side of the dale – a collection of houses grouped around a green, the whole situated on a gravel delta above the floodplain of the River Skirfare.

The name Arncliffe is said to be derived from erne [white-tailed sea eagle] which presumably nested on the limestone cliff providing a dramatic backdrop. M'duke Miller, mine host of "The Falcon", used to talk about Amerdale, the old name of the valley. Wordsworth had written about "the deep fork of Amerdale". M'duke's widow lives at Bridge End, a house visited by Charles Kingsley, the Devonian who became Rector of Eversley in Hampshire and who (as related when I passed through Malhamdale) knew the Yorkshire Dales well.

Kingsley was in the Dales with his family in 1863. "The Water-Babies", his best-known work, was partly inspired by the scenery in the Malham and Arncliffe districts, and written for the delight of his son, Grenville, being described as "a Fairy Tale for a Land-Baby". It appeared in print as a series in a magazine until, its popularity assured, the work was published as a book.

Kingsley is said to have visited little old Miss Hammond at Bridge End and she featured in the book. While chatting with Mary Miller, the present occupant of the house, I was shown a photograph of that same Miss Hammond.

From the hill path to Kettlewell I saw Littondale blend with Wharfedale. The Skirfare and the Wharfe join their waters at "Amerdale Dub". Kettlewell was the home of C.J. Cutliffe Hyne, who wrote entertaining stories about Captain Kettle. He startled the natives in the

1930s by going panning for gold in local streams. Cutliffe Hyne actually found some, but not in in a quantity sufficient to repay him for his efforts.

An ancestor of my wife, Matthew Bell, who was a farmer's son at Kettlewell, was converted by the Mormons; he went to Liverpool and sailed across the Atlantic to the mouth of the Missouri, continuing with a wagon train across Injun Country and noting, in a letter home, that the wagons were arranged in a circle at night because the Indians were inclined to steal livestock.

I thought of this ordinary Wharfedale lad and his new life in Salt Lake City as I strode through Kettlewell and took to the hills again. Now I was following a path at the edge of the moor ("tewit grund"), where lapwings were flying sorties against crows.

I descended to Conistone (an Anglian name, meaning "farmstead of cows"), using a route within sight of The Pie (a cairn) and Wassa Hill (with its television mast). Conistone which, like Arncliffe, is situated on a gravel bed, has a pleasantly open appearance, an effect created by green spaces.Town children whooped and shrieked at the Methodist Chapel, which now has the dual role of a place of worship and a hostel.

I walked through the dry valley of Gurling Trough on my way to Conistone Dib. The mini-ravine had been carved out by the furious rush of meltwater from snow and ice which had lain like a deep crust on the fells. I could not take the Trough in at a glance, for it went this way and that, rather than in a direct line. At one point, this limestone ravine narrowed to a few feet.

I slithered on smooth grey stones. The path led into a wider, sunlit valley – a place of screes and, in spring, of floral blooms – yellow mountain pansy, tormentil, milkwort and violet.

I turned right, towards Yarnbury, and was welcomed to the high pastures by more lapwings which were showing off their flying skill. I crossed the Dales Way long-distance path and negotiated a couple of stiles, one of them situated near a copse which off-set the otherwise empty appearance of the landscape.

The views were extensive, taking in the reef-knolls around Thorpe and, just over the Lancashire border, the distinctive "ridge tent" appearance of Pendle Hill, where the witches are supposed to live (their homes lay a little to the south of the eminence).

Westward, and closer at hand, was Bastow Wood, above Grass Wood, and nearby I saw the gleam from limestone pavements. Bare House, the hilltop farmstead near which I walked, had seen better days, as "they" say. Indeed, this place has also been known as Barras, from the Norse bargh-hus, or hill farm. It was the Ordnance Surveyors who misheard the name or misread the records and rendered the farm "Bare".

At Limekiln Lane, high walls acted as "blinkers", restricting my views. Hearing a miscellany of excited grouse calls, I peered through a gap in the wall and saw two cock birds spoiling for a fight. The birds moved side by side, calling all the while. The crowing took on an urgent, gutteral manner.The birds, now bubbling over with fervour, and having run out of diplomatic moves, scuffled, fluttering against each other in a shower of displaced body feathers.

And so I came to the tortured ground of Yarnbury, looking (without the need of much effort) for the traces of lead-mining days. Spoil heaps sterilised the ground. Light was reflected back from dams large and small. Water glinted in the Duke of Devonshire's Watercourse.

At what remains of the Cupola Smelt Mill, built in 1793 by the Duke's men, to replace the original peat-and-wood-burning mill, lead mining activity was formalised from 1603 by miners from Derbyshire. In the late 18th century, shallow shafts were succeeded by much deeper workings as the mining process became mechanised.

Cottages at Buckden (Marilyn White).

Kilnsey Crag and village (G. Dodd).

Kettlewell village and church (Dez Wilson).

I followed the Duke's New Road to where the partly collapsed flue of the smelt mill led me to a chimney on the skyline which was splendidly restored in 1966.

Arthur Raistrick has written about the large number of horses that would be needed at Yarnbury to bring peat to the smelt mill and to take away lead to the marketing centres of Pateley Bridge and Skipton. When, in about 1760, some 600 tons of smelted lead a year had to be shifted, each ton would require at least eight horses. It is calculated that about 7,000 horse loads of mined and dressed ore, and some 5,000 horse loads of lead, were involved.

By the 1850s, these developments had raised production to around 1,200 tons of lead per annum and the mines employed up to 200 men and boys. The exhaustion of existing mines led to a rapid decline of the industry. Eventually, with the importation of cheap lead from abroad, it was no longer worth while to prospect for further veins. The mining had ended by 1882.

Yarnbury achieved a special kind of fame when emissaries of Paramount Pictures arrived with plans to build Wuthering Heights, the farmhouse created in the vivid imagination of Emily Bronte, at a moorside site.

Those who saw it marvelled. It appeared that a mansion had been built on the moor-edge. In fact, it was a facade, of wood and moulded plaster, held firmly in place by scaffolding. The old gate stoops on the way to the house – stoops which, like mushrooms, appeared overnight – were on a wooden frame. One man could carry each of them away.

A field barn was embellished with a tower and porch. For the purposes of filming, it became a church. In a nearby field, plaster gravestones were set (with no hummocks to represent the graves themselves) and as soon as the men knocked off for a meal, the moor sheep moved in and began to use the "gravestones" as scratching-posts.

One item of equipment I did not see used was the "wind machine". A real Bronte wind moaned about the district during filming; it threatened to bring "Wuthering Heights" clattering down but the men had built it well.

11

GRASSINGTON
AND SIMON'S SEAT

While sitting in the cobbled Square at Grassington, I recall the life and witness of John Crowther, chemist and antiquary. I use a field route to Elbolton and continue, over innumerable stiles, to Burnsall. At Parcevall Hall, I discover how brains and brass can convert an old farmstead into an architectural showplace. I brave the heights of Simon's Seat.

Memories crowded on me as I descended from Yarnbury to Grassington. There was the time a local worthy named Sam Stables reported to "The Craven Herald and Pioneer" that an albino carrion crow had been seen in the district.

When the news item did not appear, Sam went out and shot the bird, leaving it at the "Herald" office, where – this being wartime, with food rationing in force – it was mistaken by the advertisement manager for a gift of something edible from a farmer.

A visit to the well-stocked museum reminded me of tales I had heard of John Crowther, a local antiquary. He was the man who put together that strange little guide book known as "Silver Garrs". As a chemist in Main Street he sold photographic equipment and also produced mineral waters, paying local boys a penny a session for pedalling an appliance to power the necessary machinery. Crowther was known as "John Pop".

He was a founder member of the electricity company which installed a turbine on the Wharfe below Grassington Bridge. He had his own museum. And this "wonderful person" left instructions in his will that on his death a certain Thomas Pickles, who ran a small carriers' business, with horse and wagon, should take him in his coffin from his home at Grassington, thence by Grass Woods to Conistone Churchyard for burial. His instructions were carried out to the letter.

Grassington is yet another Wharfedale village with an Anglian foundation but it grew lustily with the lead-mining period. The old part of town has many former miners' cottages that are now much-sort-after accommodation for retired couples.

The parish church lies across the Wharfe at Linton. My walk led me into yet another Anglian-founded settlement with a green, though the houses I saw were mainly of the 17th and 18th century.

The beck carried the obligatory tame mallard, which mob visitors. I saw the White Abbey (which has no monastic connections) where Halliwell Sutcliffe, a writer with a romantic style, wrote novels. He was the author of "The Striding Dales", which though fanciful in places has hardly ever been out of print since it was penned.

Dominating the village green is the Fountaine Hospital, founded and endowed in 1721 by Richard Fountaine, who wished its benefits to be conferred on "six poor men or women". As Richard acquired timber for none other than Sir John Vanbrugh, it is possible that this "hospital" was built to a grand design by that famous architect.

A field path led to Thorpe, the "hidden hamlet", which Sutcliffe's imagination peopled with cobblers. I followed a walled track to Elbolton, the best known of the Wharfedale reef knolls. On the dry hillside, I tried to picture the area as it was 330 million years ago, when this was a coral reef in a clear sea with attendant sea-lilies, algae and sponges, traces of

Yarnbury, near Grassington.

Grassington's main street and Town Hall.

which can be found in the rocks at various elevations on the hillside.

Elbolton was extensively excavated by miners looking for mineral riches. A few natural caves were found and in 1889 one of them, which was entered by a shaft, yielded human skeletons buried in a crouched position and also Neolithic pottery. The bones of bears were also collected.

If you read Dixon, a writer about Craven folklore, you will discover that Elbolton is a fascinating place to visit by moonlight, when the "little people" are dancing. You might be invited to join in the dance!

On the way to Burnsall, I had a fellow feeling with a horse directed round the Grand National course, for over a dozen stiles set in walls were to be negotiated. My legs creaked with effort by the time I came to Badger Lane, named after one of the old-time pedlars who wandered about the Dales with necessities.

At Burnsall, I felt to be on a frontier between two worlds. I was about to leave behind the limestone country, with its scars and dry valleys, its free-draining turf and pastel shades, to enter a gritstone landscape, as reflected in heavier soils, in the brown of the walls and a profusion of heather on the hills.

I found a spare seat on Burnsall green and fed the ducks, meanwhile glancing at the river bridge, which was repaired and beautified in 1612 by Sir William Craven, the Dick Whittington of Craven, so called because he "made good" in London but did not forget his native village, founding a grammar school just below the church, where this generous man is commemorated by a tablet in the south aisle.

Another unusual person to made his mark on upper Wharfedale was Sir William Milner, an architect, who transformed a Dales farm and its environs. I walked by Hartlington and Appletreewick to Skyrethorne, here to visit Parcevall Hall.

Sir William, during a walking trip to Wharfedale in the early 1920s, saw a farm which was referred to on the 1909 Ordnance Survey map as Percival Hall. It clung to a southward-facing hillside at an elevation of almost 1,000 ft. Around it were meadows, some sheep-folds and a few ash trees.

William Milner, this tall, wealthy bachelor, a godson of Queen Mary and brother-in-law of Lord Linlithgow, became 8th Baronet of Nun Appleton Hall near York. He was a partner in a York architectural practice. Buying the Wharfedale farm, he set about transforming it and re-named it Parcevall Hall.

In a few hectic years, assisted by teams of men, horses and carts – and at a cost said to be in the region of £40,000 – he transformed the extensive buildings, intending that they should regain something of their old Elizabethan character. Two wings were added, using well-weathered material from an old barn and a derelict house purchased at Bewerley, near Pateley Bridge. Six acres of ground were turned into gardens and woodland.

A deeply religious man, Sir William created a small chapel, in which he placed a statue of Our Lady of Walsingham. The chapel is so small there was room only for a priest, for the owner and Bracken, his Labrador dog.

In his later years, taxation bit deeply into his resources, or he would most likely have transformed Trollers Ghyll, a limestone ravine, by flooding part of it. He had intended to plant the land round about with rhododendron, such as the species introduced into England by his good friend Reginald Farrer, of Clapham. A tract of woodland just outside the main grounds at Parcevall was known to Sir William as "Little Tibet".

He gave Parcevall Hall and estate to Walsingham and they are leased at a peppercorn rent to the Diocese of Bradford as a retreat and conference centre. The gardens are "open

Grassington, from the top of the main street (D. Mark Thompson).

Burnsall church and grammar school.

to view" at prescribed times.

Having arrived at Parcevall in the springtime, I was fascinated to learn how Sir William planted his daffodil bulbs. He collected everyone who might help, including an upholsterer who arrived at the Hall to cover some chairs. Sir William then filled a large sack with bulbs, tied it loosely and, walking through the orchard, swung the sack around his head. The bulbs flew out and wherever they landed they must be planted. So they were planted at random rather than in disciplined rows.

I took the zig-zag way from Skyreholme to the summit of Simon's Seat. And up there, in the dampness and mist which swirled around weathered gritstone, I was back in the now familiar world of peat, heather and red grouse.

Our romantic writer, Halliwell Sutcliffe, referred to this modest summit as "a sheer rock-fortress guarding these virile lands". It was Sutcliffe who related the fanciful story of a shepherd who found a baby boy lying in a wicker basket, "sheltered by the rocks from sun or storm".

Simon tucked the child under his coat for warmth and took him to the wife of a fellow shepherd. Now read on...

"Soon afterwards, the Barden shepherds met in conclave. They put each a little from their meagre earnings to the common fund, and reared the bairn between them, and he was known as Simon Amang 'em, because Simon the shepherd found him first, and because the others shared his maintenance.

"The Amanghams, a family scattered wide to-day, go to the books and the Heralds' College for the meaning of their name. They should come instead to this rugged scarp of rock that gives its simple name..."

Using the front door of the "sheer rock-fortress" of Simon's Seat, I entered the romantic world of mid-Wharfedale.

12

BARDEN
AND BOLTON

I meet an aggressive pheasant in the Valley of Desolation, and listen to the warble of a dipper by the Wharfe while touring the classic landscape of Bolton and Barden. A moorland way leads me to Rylstone Cross. I complete my circular walk by trudging through Winterburn to Malham.

I shared my snack with a cock pheasant. Having descended from Simon's Seat into the Valley of Desolation (which is no longer desolate), I sat near the principal waterfall and opened my plastic food container. A pheasant which had simply been a decorative part of the scene dashed towards me and almost knocked the box from my hands.

For several minutes, I tried to push the bird away, but it regarded my box as just another food-hopper. So I tossed the pheasant a sandwich, followed by a cake. When its curiosity was exhausted and its hunger assuaged, I continued my walk into the classic countryside of mid-Wharfedale.

"Valley of Desolation" is the romantic title for what is really Posforth Gill, and you cannot find a more unglamorous name than that. In 1826, a storm ravaged the area, topping trees like dominoes. Needless to say, the Valley has since recovered. The inevitable conifer plantation has appeared but elsewhere trees have been planted to arrest some erosion.

The old oaks, grand-daddies all, have young companions in the stripling oaks – a gift by the Ramblers' Association – planted by the estate and growing behind sheep-proof barriers. It was sad to see that Dutch Elm disease had gained entry and was engaged in its specialist form of devastation.

One old warrior oak lying on its side bore a carving by some lovesick swain. Frederic Montagu, in 1838, riled against those who cut their initials on the trees. He asserted: "Let me earnestly entreat these young aspirants in the art of carving in wood, to recollect that they are upon private property, and though allowed a temporary lodging, their board [this word being emphasised] is not included."

Hereabouts was the Deer Park, last used as such just before the 1914-18 war. Some years ago, I tracked down Bolton deer antlers to the Hall and Barden Tower. Few people now remember the last of the Wharfedale reds.

The deer were not emparked simply to adorn the landscape. A deer park was, to a medieval lord, a protein bank. If there was anything which medieval people yearned for in mid-winter it was to sink their teeth into good red meat, for that was the time when food was scarce and any preserved meat had been sunk in brine.

Some of the veteran oaks, though hollow, still manage to produce a sprig or two of greenery in spring. Perhaps one or two were saplings almost 1,000 years ago. Could it be – as Arthur Raistrick once suggested to me – that the oldest were alive in pre-Norman days?

Bolton Priory retained its unhurried, contemplative atmosphere. Here, in a fertile pocket between the moors, the former nave, splendidly cared for, serves as the parish church and the rest is in its romantically ruined state, though without the climbing ivy which was beloved of old-time poets and artists.

It was annoying to see that since the footbridge across the river had been attended to, a

The ruined east end of Bolton Priory.

Chapel House, Barden Tower.

concrete sill had canalised the Wharfe and covered the old stepping stones. Photographers may now capture the reflection of the Priory in the water.

Wordsworth, who incorporated a somewhat bloodthirsty story relating to the Norton family in his long poem about the White Doe of Rylstone wrote: "From Bolton's old monastic tower/The bells ring loud with gladsome power". Halliwell Sutcliffe, equally effusive, mentioned "the grace of her, the pensive charm, are bosomed in a wonderland that could happen nowhere else" (ugh!). Nathaniel Hawthorne saw the ruined Priory "in the green lap of protecting hills, beside a stream and with peace and fertility looking down on every side".

A small boy, beholding the ruins, said to his mother: "Did the monks build this place?" She nodded. There was a moment's contemplation, and he observed: "Haven't they left it untidy?"

It is not easy to write about Bolton Priory without being romantic, but I will try. In 1125, Cecily, who had married William Meschin, established a church of regular canons of the order of St. Augustine at Embsay.

It was Alice who made it possible for the canons to move to the more sheltered site of Bolton 35 years later. One of those who witnessed the document was her son, the Boy of Egremond, though a story persists that the Priory owes its foundation to the act of a grieving mother when the Boy was drowned at The Strid.

In its heyday, the Priory had 26 canons and employed about 200 lay workers at Bolton and on the far-flung monastic estate. Generally, the history of the Priory was uneventful. One shattering exception occurred in 1315, with the appearance of marauding Scots. They caused so much damage that the Priory had to be evacuated, with the exception of those few who maintained the continuity of worship.

Even more shattering was the Dissolution. Prior John Moone walled off the Nave, which was thus retained as the parish church. The Priory gatehouse is incorporated in Bolton Hall, where the Duke of Devonshire and his family stay on their visits to Yorkshire.

The area between Bolton and Barden Bridges was beloved of English painters, including Girton, Cotman, Turner and Cox. When an art exhibition was held at the "Devonshire Arms" some years ago, one of the organisers, Francis Kyle, saw this part of Wharfedale as a "slightly manicured" landscape. It gave gave the impression of being carefully preserved.

From the 1720s, prompted by the new enthusiasm for the aesthetics of travel which would develop into tourism, the painters transformed what had been a topographical genre into a landscape art.

In the 18th century, Bolton Abbey could be reached by good coach roads. The number of visitors peaked between 1793 and 1815, when the Napoleanic Wars made the Grand Tour of the Continent impracticable. People "of taste and means" awoke to the existence of grand country in Britain.

Landseer made sketches for his romantic painting "Bolton Abbey in the Olden Time". He was his usual flamboyant self – wearing his favourite maroon shooting coat and, at one time, setting up his easel in the river!

The large painting he produced did not relate specifically to Bolton Priory. It might have been painted anywhere. The outdoors is represented by the merest patch of sky. The rest consists of a general purposes religious setting, with monastic officials receiving, from the tenantry, various items of food including the body of a stag, a large trout and a variety of birds, including bittern and swan.

The painting, exhibited at the Royal Academy in 1834, encouraged yet more visitors to Bolton Abbey (as the village had become known). King George V arrived for the grouse-

Barden Tower (Alec Wright).

Bolton Bridge (E.C. Clark).

shooting. On Sunday, he walked from Bolton Hall to the Priory Church to attend worship. He was recalled by a native as "a littleish fellow with gingery whiskers; a gruff sort of man, but kind to children."

This monarch was, by all accounts, a crack shot. "He used to bring his pony with him. It was a white 'un called Jock." His love of children was demonstrated one Sunday when he noticed that the police were keeping back a crowd of sightseers. The King said the children must be allowed to come nearer.

King George VI, on a tour of the North during the 1939-45 war, stopped at Bolton Abbey station, where a special air raid shelter had been constructed "in the banking". After the war, this Royal shelter was used by a local man as a storage place for his gardening equipment.

The path from the Cavendish Pavilion to the Strid was as I remembered it of old – broad, dry, pounded into concrete hardness by thousands of visitors. The Strid Woods had kept their old-time lushness of grass, flower and leaf. In summer, this part of Wharfedale is extravagantly green, flavoured by garlic, heady with bird song.

A dipper warbled while standing on a rounded stone by the river. When the short, hard song was over, the bird "courtseyed" several times, drawing attention to the white "bib" on its dark brown plumage. The dipper then waded in the shallows, looking for insect food on the bed of the river.

This Dales water-sprite moved restlessly, one moment wading and in another moment swimming. The dipper perched on a boulder, then jumped into the river and vanished from sight, continuing its quest for food among the stones and exploiting a specialist niche in the bird world.

The Wharfe is a "flashy" river, which quickly rises and quickly falls, as it handles storm-water from much higher up the dale. I have known days when storms have grumbled around the fells and Bolton Abbey has been dry and sunny.

An estate workman showed me a notch cut in a rock 15 ft. above the normal level of the river, marking a high water level in 1936. He quoted a familiar old couplet:

> *Wharfe is clear, and Aire is lyth,*
> *Where the Aire drowns one, Wharfe drowns five.*

The Strid Woods, which cover about 130 acres, on both sides of the Wharfe, are sheltered and damp, which results in a micro-climate in which trees grow well. At times, when vapour is rising from the river, enveloping the trees, the woodland resembles a tropical rain forest.

The area is managed as a much appreciated amenity rather than on strictly commercial lines. Here was a happy hunting ground of Victorian naturalists. The Wharfedale Naturalists' Society, based on Ilkley, is active in recording plants and bird life.

Some 50 species of bird breed in the area. This is one of the relatively few places in Yorkshire where the pied flycatcher, a summer migrant which arrives towards the end of April, has a breeding haunt. The goosander, here at the southern edge of its British breeding range, nests in hollow trees.

At The Strid, I watched the river flowing silently between gritstone banks. The dark, bubbling water was like boiling treacle. The flanking grit is a coarse sandstone containing among the quartz grains a proportion of feldspar and some pebbles. These are – so the experts say – "the earliest rocks of the Upper Carboniferous Series, E-zone" and they are some 325 million years old.

The rocks are horizontal. The rotary action of pebbles in the rapid current of the river when in flood has created potholes. Small potholes point upstream and large ones are shaped like corkscrews. Indeed, this gorge was formed from the joining up of a succession of potholes over a period of time we would find it difficult to comprehend.

I shared The Strid with a group of walkers on the Dales Way. Those young people, who were en route from Ilkley to Bowness, had reason to thank the Rev William Carr, Rector of Bolton Priory from 1789 to 1843, who – with the approval of the Duke of Devonshire – arranged for the creation of "close on 30 miles of walks", none of them being severe.

Sightseeing in Victorian times was orderly. Seats were position according to the best views. The seats were named after members of the Duke's family and friends and include Lady Harriet and Lady Georgina.

Wordsworth commended Mr Carr's efforts. In devising the network of paths, he had worked "with an invisible hand of art – in the very spirit of nature". It is believed that Sir Joseph Paxton designed Strid Cottage. Was he also responsible for the old (disused) toilet block, a stone building, with slate roof and a porch as a sort of waiting area? Inside this toilet were two seats, side by side.

An advantage of a woodland trail is that crowds can be dispersed throughout it without giving the impression of crowding. There are intervening trees – beech (some with an age of 350 years), oak, syacamore (including some with a curly grain) and alder in the wettest places.

In spring, the open ground is speckled by wood anemone, wood sorrel, lesser celandine, primrose, drifts of bluebells and much else. Sweet Ciceley flavours its growing area with the strong smell of aniseed.

I walked by the river to where an aqueduct provided a handy crossing point. The path I followed led me to Barden and a handsome bridge – a narrow but strong bridge, well buttressed against the excesses of the river. In 1673, Barden and six other bridges spanning the Wharfe were carried away. Three years later, Barden bridge had been "repared" at the charge of the whole West Riding.

The road climbed to where Barden Tower stood in the (romantically) ruined state in which it has been since early last century. The building, replacing the old hunting lodge of the Cliffords, was built by Henry, the "Shepherd Lord" who had been brought up by shepherds in the Lake District.

He was a man with a strong curiosity who, having returned to his family's estate in Yorkshire, and providing himself with comfortable quarters at Barden, which he preferred to his castle at Skipton, applied himself to the study of alchemy and astrology. In the year 1513, when Henry was 60 years old, he led a party of Craven men to join the English army which routed the Scots at Flodden Field, in Northumberland.

A halberd said to have been used at Flodden was to be seen in Chapel House, beside the Tower, though Arthur Raistrick used to claim it was merely an item surviving from the Tower's armoury.

From Barden I crossed the Moor – with more crowing grouse to entertain me – to where one of the big reservoirs built by Bradford had caught the eye of the afternoon sun. I trudged by Hutchen Gill Head and Brown Bank to reach Rylstone Cross, on its gritstone ridge.

From Hetton the way led north-westwards, passing near Winterburn Reservoir to attain Weets Cross, yet another monastic marker, but in this case one where a stone shaft remains on the base.

I walked down to Malham, between drystone walls and spring-green fields, within hearing of lark, curlew and raucous day-tripper. My Dales excursion, which had begun on a golden evening by Malham Cove, ended in the village under a cornflower-blue sky.